THE
MENTALLY ILL CHILD
GROWS UP

TRANSITIONS TO THE WORLD OF WORK

THE
MENTALLY ILL CHILD GROWS UP

TRANSITIONS TO THE WORLD OF WORK

BERTRAM J. BLACK

Professor Emeritus
Departments of Psychiatry,
Epidemiology, and Social Medicine
Albert Einstein College of Medicine

BRUNNER/MAZEL *Publishers* • NEW YORK

HV
3005
, B53
1994

Library of Congress Cataloging- in-Publication Data

Black, Bertram J.
   The mentally ill child grows up : transitions to the world of work / by Bertram J.
Black.
        p.   cm.
   Includes bibliographical references and index.
   ISBN 0-87630-711-X
   1. Mentally ill—Employment—United States. 2. Mentally ill children—
Education—United States. 3. Mentally ill children—Services for—United States. I.
Title.
   [DNLM: 1. Mental Disorders—in adolescence. 2. Rehabilitation, Vocational.
3. Employment. 4. Vocational Education. WS 463 B627m 1993]
HV3005.B53 1993
362.2'0425—dc20
DNLM/DLC
for Library of Congress   93-31218
                                                                              CIP

Published by
BRUNNER/MAZEL, INC.
19 Union Square West
New York, New York 10003

Manufactured in the United States of America
10 9 8 7 6 5 4 3 2 1

To
BRUCE, PAUL, AND ANNE

CONTENTS

PREFACE

This book is the result of two sets of experiences. In one of these, at three times in my professional life I have wrestled with the problems of developing programs for the transition of emotionally disturbed young people into adult working roles. The first of these was as the director of an institution for dependent and delinquent children and adolescents; the second was while in charge of a vocational rehabilitation center that pioneered in serving people who were mentally ill; the third was while directing rehabilitation services for a state campus of hospitals for the mentally ill, both adults and children, and for the mentally retarded/developmentally disabled. These attempts, however, took place long before the advent of the Education for All Handicapped Children Act of 1975 (P.L. 94-142).

I must admit that, at best, those programs for the transition of adolescents to adult working roles were only partially successful. Among the complications I experienced in designing such services was the problem of integrating programs between the various human service fields (e.g., education, social services, labor-manpower, mental health, mental retardation). It was also difficult to effect a common understanding among the disciplines involved (psychiatry, psychology, education, social work, vocational counseling, and others). There was no single objective, such as the 1975 federal legislation and its outcomes seem now to be achieving.

The more recent experience that stimulated this manuscript grew out of research for my book Work and Mental Illness: Transitions to Employment. In visits to programs, experiments, and demonstrations across the country I was pleased, and sometimes impressed, to find services under a variety of auspices targeted toward assisting youngsters who are handicapped/disabled make the transition to the adult world of work. An increasing number of these were obviously serving emotionally disturbed or mentally ill young people. However, there seemed to be little communication between these ventures, and programs in one locale or in one set of human services knew little of what was being tried elsewhere. There is a current ferment of activity toward increasing communication and disseminating information, focused on people who are disabled and the programs that serve them, stimulated by the federal Office of Special Education and Rehabilitative Services, U. S. Department of Education, and hopefully this will result in more and better programs for young disabled persons, especially for the mentally ill and emotionally disturbed.

With the current developments in education for those who are handicapped, and with reawakened interest in psychiatric rehabilitation, I believe there is need for a summation of fact and policy as applied to transitional services for mentally ill, emotionally and behaviorally disturbed adolescents, for these youngsters all too frequently fall between the cracks in mental health and in educational services. Certainly those who work in the mental health professions should understand the current scene, and those who serve such youngsters educationally could benefit by an overview. While the literature is rapidly increasing on all facets of care, education, and treatment, I have not come across any other attempt to present the picture in toto.

I am most grateful to the many persons in psychiatric services and special educational programs for adolescents and young adults who have supplied information for this book, who have shown me programs, and who have advised and taught me. I owe particular thanks to Dr. Joseph S. Lechowicz and Dr. Peter Stastny for reviewing sections of the manuscript, and to Dr. E. Richard Feinberg and Mr. Aaron Burger who critiqued the whole. I am indebted to the van Ameringen Foundation for supporting the fact gathering and to the Medical and Health Research Association of New York City for sponsoring the writing. I appreciate the capable assistance of my wife at every stage of this work. Any errors of fact are mine alone, as are opinions about programs and relation to psychiatric and other human service programs and to policy and economics.

FOREWORD

Mental health practitioners and other professionals working with disturbed children and adolescents tend to retreat when their patients or clients begin the approach to adulthood, particularly when the transition to the world of work becomes imminent. This is unfortunate because it is during this time that the aging mentally ill adolescent, who may be just beginning to do quite nicely in mastering the tasks and attendant stresses of the period, may again destabilize, sometimes markedly, requiring (re)-hospitalization or at least a level of care greater than needed by more normal adolescents.

Part of the reluctance of professionals to become or to remain involved in their charges' transitions undoubtedly is related to the enormous complexity of the several systems that must articulate properly in order to fashion appropriate, individualized programs for clients, balancing client specificity with general applicability.

As the reader will discover in this book, Professor Black does not retreat, avoid, ignore, or otherwise eschew the myriad interstices created by the interaction or lack of interaction beween the myriad systems. Rather, he is eager to survey, discuss, and integrate information—including what others would discard, or not bother with at all—into a broad (re)-habilitative fabric that covers the feelings of functional nakedness and of overscrutiny and overself-scrutiny so often experienced by youngsters struggling to enter the work arena at the same time they are struggling not to enter it.

This book is designed for trained and aspiring professionals alike in any of the fields invoved in the transitional process.

For those already trained but slightly rusty in their areas of principal endeavor (e.g., child-adolescent development, child-adolescent mental health/illness, vocational (re)-habilitation, etc.) the basics are clearly defined in modern terminology. And for professionals-to-be the material will also be most instructive because of its clarity and open manner of presentation.

The Mentally Ill Child Grows Up: Transitions to the World of Work is a welcome addition to the literature in this area. But it is not merely an addition to the field; it is, because of its breadth and depth, a very unique contribution, surely to be helpful to the helpers of the youngsters who are the subject of it.

E. RICHARD FEINBERG, M.D.

Executive Director,
Bronx Children's Psychiatric Center;
Professor of Psychiatry,
Director, Division of Child and
Adolescent Psychiatry,
Department of Psychiatry,
Albert Einstein College of Medicine,
Bronx, NY

THE
MENTALLY ILL CHILD
GROWS UP

TRANSITIONS TO THE WORLD OF WORK

CHAPTER 1

INTRODUCTION AND OVERVIEW

Although the literature on mental illness is replete with descriptions and analyses of its manifestations in childhood and in adulthood, there is much less information about the in-between years of adolescence. There is professional and scientific interest in adolescence per se, but little to be found on the transition of those who are mentally ill/emotionally disturbed from the status of "child" to that of "adult." For all youngsters the years from late adolescence to young adulthood are complicated by, in addition to personal and family psychological matters, the ending of legally required schooling, the economics of separation from family, the onset of independent living, and the need to assume the mantle of "worker" or "wage earner" or otherwise to become a self-dependent contributor to the gross national product.

In recent years much interest has developed in the problems of children with disabilities in their transition from school to work. However, the focus has been on children with physical handicaps or with mental retardation and/or developmental disabilities. A more recent concern has been with "learning-disabled" children, but there is little in the literature about programs for emotionally disturbed or mentally ill young-sters. This is not to say there are no such programs, for quite a number of services identified as exemplary in providing transitions from school to work for disabled young people list the emotionally disturbed among their reported clientele.

This monograph describes the current state of operation of such services, specifies the needs of the youngsters requiring services, and suggests the configuration of programs and services that would appear to meet these needs most nearly.

THE EXTENT OF NEED

The Midtown Study of mental illness in the U. S. population (Srole, 1962) suggested that some 5% to 10% of the school children had psychiatric ailments sufficient to have warranted a psychiatric diagnosis. In the quarter century since that study, it has been generally believed that this proportion has not decreased; in fact, in part because of the baby boom following World War II, the number of emotionally disturbed children in the population has more than likely increased. A recent report in the *New York Times* stated that "as many as one in five children suffer from psychiatric problems serious enough to impair their lives in "some way" (Goleman, 1989; see also Brandenburg et al., 1989). It is difficult to make any precise measurement of emotional disturbance/mental illness. The terms are not very specific and are used differently in various settings. What the educator calls "emotional disturbance" may not yield a psychiatric diagnosis at all; and a child who is in fact psychiatrically ill may be adjudged "learning disabled" by the teacher.(see, for example, Raffali, 1990). As Behar (1984) explained:

> The definitions of the targeted child population continue to be blurred. The terminology shifts easily from mentally ill to emotionally disturbed to behaviorally disturbed to troubled children to children in trouble. In truth, many of the children have behavioral problems, learning problems, and family problems and frequently have been in legal trouble as well. Most of the children to be served do not neatly divide themselves in the way administrative agencies have been created. (p. 1)

In 1989 the Institute of Medicine (IOM) estimated that the number of children in the United States who may be suffering from mental illness is between 11 and 14 million, only 20% to 33% of whom are under appropriate mental health care (NARF, 1989). Recently, headquarters staff members of the New York City Board of Education estimated that out of 125,000 children in the school system known to be handicapped, some 20% are "emotionally disturbed," 70% are "learning disabled," and the rest are "mentally retarded" or physically disabled. The comparable figures for New York State for 1984-85 were 45% "learning disabled" and 16% "emotionally disturbed" (New York State Council, 1987).

The advent in 1975 of the Education for All Handicapped Children Act, Public Law 94-142, brought attention to the numbers and types of handicapped youngsters requiring education. Concern arose immediately for those children who were facing obstacles in school or whose handicaps made it difficult for them to attend school. Parents and organizations concerned with the mentally retarded/developmentally disabled and the physically disabled pressed for special attention, followed by those whose children could be called learning disabled. A variety of programs ensued, linking regular curricula with special classes and remedial programs for handicapped children, with vocational education playing a commanding role in the secondary schools.

The Reagan administration's call for developing programs aiding in the transition of handicapped youngsters from school to work resulted in an increasing number of experiments and demonstrations in school systems and rehabilitation programs, and between them. Although many of these claim to serve emotionally disturbed youngsters, their primary emphasis is on those with disabilities in general, on the learning disabled, or on the mildly and moderately mentally retarded.

It is by no means clear what is meant by "emotional disturbance" in these demonstrations, except that children referred through the public school systems are subject to "labeling" in the development of Individualized Education Programs (IEP), as required by the federal law. With regard to emotional and mental illness, it should be understood that while a focus on the "severely mentally ill" among the adult population is on those suffering from the major psychoses and affective disorders, the problems of secondary school pupils are mainly disorders of adjustment, impulse control, and personality.

Children with a diagnosis of schizophrenia or major depressive symptoms are not likely to be found in the regular school system. They are usually in psychiatric institutions or under outpatient care, receiving special schooling or none at all. Also, schizophrenic breakdowns usually occur in the late adolescent years or early twenties, after secondary schooling has been completed, interfering with higher education or with entrance into the job world. The incidence of affective disorders is more frequent in later years, in the twenties or thirties, causing disturbance with working and living patterns rather than with the transition from school to work. This is not to say that manifestations of depression do not occur in schoolchildren. In fact, symptoms of depression appear to be more common among children than was previously supposed. Nevertheless, the general picture of an emotionally disturbed high school pupil is not one of hallucinations and/or delusions or severe withdrawal but rather of great compulsivity, histrionic or passive-aggressive behavior, attention deficit, and other traits of conduct disorder.

From the educational point of view, these behaviors produce inability to learn, so whatever else the psychiatric diagnosis may actually be, to the teacher these become "learning-disabled" youngsters. However, even a medical determination casts a wide net and is by no means precise. Dr. Robert B. Johnston (1987), of the Kennedy Institute for Handicapped Children, Johns Hopkins School of Medicine, pointed out that

> chronic learning insufficiencies are relatively easy to identify, categorize, and place in appropriate educational settings. . . . Learning inefficiencies, however, are more troublesome. Their diverse manifestations and multiple causes make them difficult to classify and treat as a group. *Specific learning disabilities* occur in one or several academic areas despite normal intelligence and adequate learning opportunities. The incapacity to attend to a learning situation in an age-appropriate way, and the subsequent manifestation, of the incapacity, are subsumed under the rubric of *attention deficit disorder* with or without hyperactivity. While it is assumed that neurological factors

play an important role in both specific learning disabilities and attention deficits, it is often difficult to document evidence of such neurological dysfunction. . . . additional confusion . . . arises when any given child with one disability manifests characteristics of the other as well. (p. 6)

A closer tie between "learning disabilities" and "emotional disturbance" is specified in the revised third edition of the *Diagnostic and Statistical Manual of Mental Disorders* (DSM-III-R, American Psychiatric Association, 1987). There, attention deficit hyperactivity disorder (ADHD) is defined as one of the mental illnesses of childhood or adolescence. The criteria for a diagnosis of ADHD follow:

A disturbance of at least six months during which at least eight of the following are present:

1. often fidgets with hands or feet or squirms in seat (in adolescents, may be limited to subjective feelings of restlessness)
2. has difficulty remaining seated when required to do so
3. is easily distracted by extraneous stimuli
4. has difficulty awaiting turn in games or group situations
5. often blurts out answers to questions before they have been completed
6. has difficulty following through on instructions from others (not due to oppositional behavior or failure of comprehension), e.g., fails to finish chores
7. has difficulty sustaining attention in tasks or play activities
8. often shifts from one uncompleted activity to another
9. has difficulty playing quietly
10. often talks excessively

11. often interrupts or intrudes on others, e.g., butts into other children's games
12. often does not seem to listen to what is being said to him or her
13. often loses things necessary for tasks or activities at school or at home (e.g., toys, pencils, books, assignments)
14. often engages in physically dangerous activities, without considering possible consequences (not for the purpose of thrill-seeking), e.g., runs into street without looking. (pp. 52-53)

The most usual onset is before the age of 6 or 7. If symptoms occur later in childhood, they are said to be most likely related to emotional factors. Common features of these symptoms are shared with conduct disorders, mental retardation, psychoses, and language disorders.

There have been estimates that ADHD occurs in 3% to 5% of children of school age (Weiss, 1976). The large numbers of children involved, and the natural desire to avoid the stigma of a label of emotional disturbance or mental illness, lend credence to the supposition that at least some—and I believe it is a large proportion of those treated as learning disabled in the educational system—are in reality emotionally disturbed youngsters. Reviews of services for transition to adulthood by "learning-disabled" adolescents in Great Britain, Denmark, the Federal Republic of Germany, the Netherlands, and Canada also indicate that emotional disturbance is included in the category (Garnett & Gerber, 1985). Therefore, in the consideration of the characteristics of programs for the transition of emotionally disturbed/mentally ill adolescents from school to work, a look at services for the learning disabled has been included.

In thinking about the issues involved in the transition from adolescence and young adulthood into the world of work of those who might be labeled mentally ill or emotionally disturbed, I find it helpful to consider the following categories separately. It should be kept in mind, however, that these are not really mutually exclusive; there is much overlap, and in individual cases it can become difficult to make an assignment.

1. Children who have dropped out of school, usually within the secondary grades, and who have now reached the age of 16 or 17 and are beyond the legally mandated age for school attendance. National surveys have reported that in 1980 12% of high school sophomores dropped out of school before their senior year. For handicapped youngsters, this figure was 22% (Rusch & Phelps, 1987).
2. Children who have been diagnosed as mentally ill and placed in mental hospitals or special schools for the mentally ill/emotionally disturbed and have now reached secondary school age.
3. Children close to or beyond the mandated school attendance age who are caught up in the correctional or penal system or who have been committed or otherwise placed in mental institutions or residential facilities.
4. Children in secondary schools, who have reached the 11th grade, and/or who may be reaching the education cutoff age of 20 or 21 years. This is by far the largest group for whom programs are planned. This is also the group that may include a goodly proportion of "learning-disabled" children.

PROGRAMS FOR SCHOOL DROPOUTS

Nationally, the first group, that of young school dropouts, is a large and troublesome one. The Center for Education Statistics reported that 14% of public high school students were identifiable as dropouts between their sophomore and senior years (Barro, 1987). For African-American students the rate was 16.8%; for Hispanics, 18.7%. More recent reports from the inner-city schools of our large urban centers show much higher figures, with percentages in the twenties and thirties. According to the New York State Education Department (1987a), "Students who come from one-parent households and large families, whose parents are relatively uneducated (especially parents who are high school dropouts themselves) are three to five times more at-risk of not completing high school than students from advantaged backgrounds" (p. 3).

Certainly, such groups include larger proportions of children with learning disabilities and emotional disturbances than do those who continue in school. In confirmation is the longitudinal study of the whole cohort of children born in 1955 on the island of Kauai, Hawaii (NIMH, 1981). Investigators made independent assessments of the children and their families and consulted community files over two decades. The study population was "a kaleidoscope of different ethnic groups, mostly non-Caucasian.... For the most part, they were immigrants from Southeast Asia and Europe who came to Hawaii to work in the sugar plantations. More than half of the children in this cohort grew up in families where the fathers were semiskilled or unskilled laborers, and many of the mothers had less than eight grades of formal education" (p. 129). At the end of the study the investigator reported:

> Roughly speaking, we could say that one out of five youngsters . . . developed serious behavior or learning problems at some time during decade one to two. For some it was because major biological insults prevented adequate development, for others it was because a persistent disorga-

nized family environment prevented normal integration, or
because several of these risk factors interacted and exposed
them to cumulative stresses which were too difficult to
cope with unaided. (p. 140)

Many of the children among the school dropout population
who do exhibit serious behavioral, mental, and/or learning
problems are institutionalized or become clients of one or
another mental health agency. If their family economics
permits, they may spend time in one of the commercial or
nonprofit residential treatment facilities. Otherwise, if they
receive community services at all, they will be found in a
public mental hospital or mental health service or they will be
caught in the juvenile or adult correctional system and be
remanded or committed by a court to a residential facility
under public or nonprofit auspices.

Generally speaking, not much attention has ever been paid
to assisting youngsters who drop out of school with attaining
entrance to the world of work. In periods when unskilled
laboring work was easily available, many of these youngsters
simply found such work. Their lack of educational attainment
did not stand in the way if their motivation, intelligence, and
social behavior were acceptable to employers. During the
Depression of the 1930s, however, it was recognized that
these attributes were insufficient to deal with the lack of work
opportunities, and the National Youth Authority, Civilian
Conservation Corps, and other work programs were set up by
the federal government both to provide work and income and
to offer training in skills that might make young people and
adults more likely to gain employment. In the 1960s presi-
dents Kennedy and Johnson used these as models to develop
manpower training programs. The Manpower Development

and Training Act of 1962 (U.S. Department of Labor, 1963) was used by President Johnson in connection with the Office of Economic Opportunity in his "War on Poverty." He developed through the federal Labor Department the Youth Opportunity Centers, Community Action Manpower Programs, the Neighborhood Youth Corps, the Job Corps, and some vocational education programs. As I have pointed out elsewhere (Black 1988):

> In the formation of these programs not much thought was given to the physically and mentally handicapped as trainees or as recipients of services. A few of the federally financed demonstrations projects for dealing with juvenile delinquency or with the community-based mentally ill, such as Mobilization for Youth, in New York City, did utilize funding from the Manpower Development and Training Act to set up what today we would call transitional employment or supported work, but these programs ceased with the end of budget authorizations.

> Not only was it difficult to organize training under an act that made no reference to coverage of the handicapped... but the U.S. Department of Labor and the Congress also kept changing the program every year or so, and what was acceptable in the regulations in one year was invalid the next. I remember, for example, running a highly acclaimed machine-shop training program for mentally ill young-adults in a sheltered workshop under U.S. Department of Labor piecework rates when a revised program required that all participants be paid one dollar an hour without regard to production. This not only removed the incentive built into our program but was illegal under our workshop certificate. The opportunities for job placement in the

private sector were thus denied to clients who required the
supportive services of the rehabilitation agency. (p. 99)

In more recent years the manpower training programs
shifted, first to the Comprehensive Employment and Training Act (CETA) in 1973 (P.L. 93-203). But it was not until
1978 that amendments to this act (P.L. 95-524) included
handicapped individuals specifically among the low-income
or unemployed persons or persons in need of training previously covered. The CETA programs differed from all of the
previous centrally controlled federal programs in that the
services and administration were through a network of state
and local units. A lot of use was made of the CETA programs
in providing training for mental hospital staff, most usually
ward aides, and for the training of paraprofessional personnel
in community clinics and agencies. However, only a limited
number of CETA programs were for work training of clientele. Such school dropouts as might have been included in
CETA services would have had to be referred from hospitals
or community agencies (Black,1988).

The Job Training Partnership Act (P.L. 97-300) replaced
CETA in 1983. This program gave even greater responsibilities to state governments; but mostly it curtailed federal funds
available for income support for trainees and for administrative costs, and severely restricted training activities in public
employment or for the kinds of work experience training
available under CETA. Authority for local planning and
management is in the hands of private industry councils rather
than local or county government. Although a number of
community agencies and some school districts have made use
of Job Training Partnership Act (JTPA) funds, for the most

part, reports indicate that much less of JTPA's resources have been available for handicapped youth or adults than was available through even the limited programs under CETA.

PROGRAMS IN MENTAL HOSPITALS OR RESIDENTIAL TREATMENT FACILITIES

The number of mentally ill or emotionally disturbed children committed, remanded, or voluntarily admitted to psychiatric children's hospitals or specialized residential centers or facilities is small in relation to the number of mentally ill/emotionally disturbed children served in special education programs. These children in the first group are the more seriously ill and handicapped. All of the psychiatric institutions for children include in their programs an educational service. Sometimes this is provided in conjunction with a local public school system, but often the institution completely controls the teaching program, either as a specially designated school of the local school district or, in the case of many state hospitals, as a separate school directly under state auspices. For example, the children's psychiatric hospitals in New York State all have school classes taught by state-certified teachers (special education). Though each "school" has a supervising teacher, analogous to a principal, the authority for administration rests with the hospital director and the responsibility and overview for planning and exercising curricula rest between a unit in the State Office of Mental Health and the State Department of Education. In contrast, one of the best known of the residential treatment facilities for disturbed and mentally ill children, Hawthorne-Cedar Knolls School, in Westchester County, New York, has its classroom teaching program designated by legislation as a Union Free School District of its own, responsible to none of the local school districts in its area. An example of a cooperative approach is the Waters Place School in the local community run by the Bronx Children's Psychiatric Center (the state hospital for children), which is supported as a special education center for outpatient children of the hospital under the New York City Board of Education.

Residential facilities for youth under the correctional system also provide for schooling. Most of this is remedial, with some vocational education thrown in. It is extremely difficult to set up an educational program for youngsters who enter the system at many levels of previous education and achievement and who may leave the system independently of educational needs. In addition, the fundamental purposes of hospitals, residential treatment centers, and psychiatric clinics are not educational, unless one takes the broad view that psychotherapy and behavioral treatment are essential educational processes. The demands of treatment appointments and other requirements of a controlled structured setting often interfere with the normal arrangements of schooling.

PROGRAMS FOR CHILDREN IN THE PUBLIC SCHOOL SETTINGS

Before the inauguration of Public Law 94-142, the Education for All Handicapped Children Act of 1975, most disabled older children in public schools who required special assistance or special services were placed in separate classes or were not in school at all. The act created

> a presumption in favor of educating children with handicaps in regular education environments.... The statute and implementing regulations require that: (1) first educational

> services appropriate for each child be defined annually in
> an Individualized Education Program (IEP), and (2) then
> an educational placement be selected from a continuum of
> alternatives so that the individually appropriate education
> can be delivered in the setting that is least removed from the
> regular education environment and that offers the greatest
> interaction with children who are not handicapped.
> (Danielson & Bellamy, 1987, p. 1)

In the decade and a half since P.L. 94-142 was enacted, there
has been a good deal of movement in many states toward such
implementation.

Danielson and Bellamy analyzed data from 50 states and
found that 26% of students with handicaps were served in
regular classes and another 44% had their programs augmented through the use of resource rooms; thus "over 70
percent of the students counted in special education spend a
substantial amount of time in regular education classes. Another 24 percent of students with handicaps are educated in
regular school buildings but are served primarily in segregated classes" (pp. 7-8). However, their analysis revealed a
great deal of variation among the states. The average state
places nearly five times as many students in segregated
settings as do the five states with the fewest students in
segregated classes. The largest proportion of the students in
such segregated settings are placed in specialized day schools.

In attending to the problems of disabled adolescents in the
public school systems, particularly those in secondary schools,
a number of approaches have been developed to deal with
graduation to adult working life. I reviewed reports of programs attested to as "exemplary," either as recipients of
demonstration grants from the federal Office of Special Education and Rehabilitation Services (OSERS) or through attes-

tation by one of the regional educational or rehabilitation networks designated by the U.S. Office of Education (see Regional Centers in references). A rough classification of these school-based programs provides three general approaches:

1. Those in which the school district acts alone to provide educational and training services for the youngsters
2. Those in which the school district actively collaborates with a work training or rehabilitation agency to provide a range of educational and work training
3. Those in which the school district collaborates with a college-based program to provide transition to higher education for those handicapped youngsters who appear to have the capabilities for college work.

School Districts Acting Alone

Most of the public school districts in this country that try to offer programs to assist handicapped secondary school students make the transition to the work world do it alone. They combine regular school classes with special education approaches and add what they have available in occupational education. They make use of such school resources as lunchrooms, libraries, clerical work, and janitorial services to provide some unpaid work experience. Sometimes nonprofit agencies, such as hospitals, charities, or museums, supply community-based work experience, and occasionally there is provision for payment to the youngsters for the work they do. Where resources are available, such as those of the federal-state vocational rehabilitation services or public employment programs, referrals may be made by the school program while the student is still in high school or, more usually, just before the student completes the schooling or reaches the cutoff age of 22.

A few examples follow:

The Community School District of Davenport, Iowa conducts the Eastern Avenue School BD (behavior disorders) Program. This is for children from ages 13 to 21, predominantly 15 to 18 years. The students have histories of academic failure, social maladjustment, delinquency, and emotional problems. The Eastern Avenue School provides a 9-month school year. Students may participate for as little as 1 year or continuously from the seventh through the 12th grade. Students are identified as behavior disordered by their local school districts according to state guidelines, and referred to the Eastern Avenue program. Treatment is based on a behavior management system. Students receive individualized attention in small classrooms. The curriculum follows state guidelines for special education. A vocational curriculum includes course work in such areas as woodworking, welding, construction, agribusiness, health, and communication and media, and classes in social skills for job seeking and job retention. Supervised unpaid work experiences are available. When students have completed their education, a Work Experience Coordinator helps in finding jobs with local businesses.

The Hillsborough County Public School District of Tampa, Florida operates the Hillsborough D.E.E.S./S.E.D. Center at the Brewster Vocational Technical Center. Students served who show aggressive behavior, poor impulse control, or poor response to authority may be withdrawn. Many have DSM-III-R diagnoses, including bipolar disorder, other affective disorders, and schizophrenia. Many were in residential treatment before entering the Center. The educational program includes the entire range of high school subjects leading toward a regular diploma, a special diploma, or the GED (general equivalency diploma) with or without certification in a trade. From the beginning of their schooling at the Center, students are placed into "real-life" work settings or into a number of adult vocational courses. A Work Experience Teacher aids in helping the student obtain work experience and later placement on a job. (These two examples were supplied by the Research and Training Center, Regional Research Institute, Graduate School of Social Work, Portland State University, Portland, Oregon.)

The New York City Board of Education set up a special education city-wide school district (District 75) to provide services for handicapped students in the 16- to 21-year age range, using federal funding under the Carl B. Perkins Vocational Education Act. The population addressed is composed primarily of learning-disabled, mildly mentally retarded, and emotionally handicapped youngsters referred by the regular school districts. Starting with the mentally retarded in the Manhattan Occupational Training Center, next the Bronx School for Career Development, and then the Manhattan School for Career Development, the latter two programs for learning-disabled and behavior-disordered youngsters, the Board of Education has used the federal funding to establish programs that could then be absorbed into the regular school system under state and local tax levy funding.

Each of these programs is referred to under the nomenclature "Project Skill." Their aim is to provide a combination of classroom remedial teaching with occupational education along with part-time job placements. Special education teachers are available at each special school; industrial arts curricula include woodshop, auto repair, electrical work, and building maintenance. Off-site teachers (mostly special education) are assigned to each of the work-training sites. Students in a group will spend part of the day on the job under the supervision of paraprofessional teaching assistants and return to the school with the teacher assistant for classroom instruction. Work experience is arranged for at hospitals, schools, nursing homes, hotels, and fast-food services and small businesses. Although the intent of the work assignments is to provide paid employment, only about one fourth of the students receive any pay. Out of 340 students participating in Project Skill at the Manhattan and Bronx Schools when I visited last year, only 85 were at jobs in which pay (usually minimum hourly wage) was available.

The California Department of Education developed three WorkAbility programs for students with handicapping conditions. WorkAbility I was piloted in 1982 and institutionalized under the Carl Perkins Vocational Education Act of 1984 (P.L. 98-524). In the school year 1986-87 the project served 342 school districts in 48 California counties. According to an independent evaluation,

> The typical WorkAbility I student is 18 years old, with a 5th-6th grade basic skills level. The ethnic composition of WorkAbility I students is similar to that reported by the State Department of Education for the general State student population. Sixty percent of the students have specific learning disabilities, 20% are seriously emotionally disturbed or mentally retarded, and 10% have severe multiple

disabilities. Half of the students are taught in resource
specialist programs and another third take part in special
day classes. (Hegenauer, 1988, pp. 1-2)

About three quarters of the students held one or more jobs
during the program. Most of these were in the clerical or sales
area; about one quarter of them were in food services, 11%
were in janitorial jobs, and 20% worked as day-care aides,
grocery clerks, or clerical aides. Earnings were close to the
minimum wage. WorkAbility staff worked with the local
school districts to organize each project. Depending on the
numbers of students involved, ranging from fewer than a
dozen to more than 300, and the local conditions, the details
of the programs varied. Where necessary, student wages were
paid from grants from WorkAbility I. In 1986-87 these
amounted to $1.4 million, or 39% of total student wages.
Private sector employers covered 42% of the wages paid, and
the rest were covered by not-for-profit agencies.

School Districts Collaborating with Rehabilitation Services

An increasing number of vocational rehabilitation agencies
serving the adult handicapped have begun to turn their attention and resources to meeting the needs of younger persons of
secondary school age. To some extent, such young people
have always been of concern to the rehabilitation services, but
on an individual, case-by-case basis. In the early 1960s, the
Jewish Vocational Services of Chicago inaugurated an
afterschool and summer program in its sheltered workshop for
handicapped high school students. Its intent was to supply a
substitute for the part-time work experiences it was assumed
that most "normal" young people had available to them

(Black, 1988). In the middle of that decade, Altro Workshops, in New York, opened its workshops to 18- to 21-year-olds in collaboration with the New York Public Employment Service (Black, 1988). These, and others like them, dealt with youngsters independently of the schooling they were receiving or had just left.

Work, Inc. One of the earliest collaborations between a rehabilitation agency and a school system took place in Massachusetts 20 years ago when Work, Inc., of Quincy, contracted with the Quincy Board of Education to supply work from its sheltered workshop to establish satellite workshops in the schools. This program has grown over the years to embrace some 25 schools in Massachusetts, and plans are under way to expand to nearby states.

Work, Inc. supplies simple assembly and packaging work on contract to the school, usually for pupil groups of 12. In 1988 the cost to each school was about $850 per month per child. This cost covered a weekly pickup and delivery of goods and merchandise and the training of a teacher (often a teacher aide) in work supervision. The supervising teacher prepares the payroll, and paychecks to the student-workers are made biweekly from Work, Inc. at piecework rates. The children are covered by work certificates from the Department of Labor, obtained by the rehabilitation agency.

A representative of Work, Inc. is invited to the meetings at the schools in which individual educational plans are determined for the handicapped children included in the program. However, there is no other contact between school curricula and the work programs for the youngsters. In recent years Work, Inc. has been developing community work programs for individual pupils referred by the schools. In these instances the school contracts with Work, Inc. for such services as employment testing, work evaluation, and case management. Testing and work trials are provided in the rehabilitation center. The youngster may then be placed in a transitional or supported work program in the community.

Participating youngsters in the programs collaborative between Work, Inc. and the school districts are about evenly divided between male and female. Children from the Boston school district are mostly Black or Hispanic; children from the other schools are almost all White. The children receive certificates of achievement at the end of the school year in which they reach age 22. Continued coverage in the Work, Inc. program is provided by the state mental health or mental retardation authority or by the Division of Rehabilitation if the student qualifies.

Work, Inc. has been gradually cutting back on its in-school sheltered work programs in favor of the community work in regular business and industry. The agency is more interested in training teachers and school districts to develop their own work-training programs. It has been difficult, however, to get interest in and understanding of the world of work on the part of special education teachers.

PERT. Another example of collaboration between school districts and vocational rehabilitation agencies is the PERT program (Postsecondary Education/Rehabilitation Center Transition) run by the Division of Special Education Programs of the Virginia Department of Education along with the Virginia Department of Rehabilitative Services and the Woodrow Wilson Rehabilitation Center (Report, 1990). PERT serves about 500 students at a time from 36 local school districts. Most of these youngsters are learning disabled or mentally retarded, but a sizable proportion is classified as emotionally disturbed. Entry to the program is usually at 16 years of age, and the students remain for 2 to 3 years, completing high school and then remaining as adult clients of the Department of Rehabilitative Services. Students are about equally divided between boys and girls, and the vast majority of them are White. Students in the PERT program remain in special education and vocational classes in their local public high schools. During high school they receive vocational services from the schools and the local school district. After they finish high school, the state vocational system for adults takes on their training in vocational or technical schools or community colleges.

School-to-Work Transition. A program that specializes in services to emotionally/behaviorally disturbed youngsters is the School-to-Work Transition for Students with Special Needs, of Rise, Incorporated, Spring Lake Park, Minnesota. This program serves six school districts represented by 10 schools. In documentation more than half of the children are learning disabled and another quarter are mentally retarded. The emotionally disturbed children are described as "not future oriented, often suicidal, and have little eligibility remaining during which they can receive assistance as children" (Report, 1990).

School District Collaboration with College-based Programs

There has been special interest in helping handicapped youngsters make the transition from secondary school to higher education. This has been particularly true for learning-disabled and for emotionally disturbed adolescents of high IQ. Three approaches are prominent: the interest of colleges (usually community colleges) in easing the way for young people who find it difficult to apply for admission or who, once admitted, need supportive measures to keep them in school; the interest of public school systems in opening the doors to higher education for disabled students who they believe have the intellectual capacity; a more recent interest by the rehabilitation field in using the "normalcy" of the college environment as preparation for adult participation in society.

WorkAbility III. Possibly the largest program in the country serving college-bound disabled youth is WorkAbility III of the California Department of Education. In this, the community colleges of the state educational system join with the state Department of Rehabilitation in providing a special program for handicapped persons aged 18 through 56. The aim is for career training, and the program reports a fairly high success rate. Job placements range from entry-level minimum wage in food service positions to professional careers. Although the California community colleges had developed a sophisticated system some years before WorkAbility III to help students with disabilities, there had been little emphasis on placement to employment. The collaboration with the Department of Rehabilitation has supplied this missing element (personal communication, Tracy, G., April 30, 1990).

Although other colleges have organized special programs to serve handicapped young persons already admitted as students, few have followed the California lead in opening the door for more easy transition from secondary schools or the community. One example of a college that did is the Fiorello H. LaGuardia Community College of the City University of New York system. This community college has developed a number of programs serving the handicapped, one of which is targeted to the learning disabled. In 1985, LaGuardia Community College launched an experimental program to assist learning-disabled young adults improve basic skills, develop work habits, and obtain a job or continue into college (personal communication, Kahn, F., May 20, 1987).

Collegebound. While all secondary schools claim to be concerned with preparing pupils for higher education, few make any special effort to assist handicapped youngsters. An example of one that does is the Winchester Public Schools, Winchester, Massachusetts. The public school offers a 13th year prep school type course for learning-disabled youngsters called its Collegebound program. A nationally recognized core curriculum is used, and students are enrolled in one course of a local community college (Collegebound, 1987).

Career Education Program. The federally supported Center for Psychiatric Rehabilitation at Boston University has developed an education program on the university campus for young adults with psychiatric disabilities as an alternative to the traditional mental health program. Known as the Career Education Program, the course of three semesters provides skill training, career planning, and a range of college curricula. An optional fourth semester allows students to work or attend other postsecondary school programs in preparation for a career. A special staff provides individual and small group instruction, supervision, and support. Opportunities for integration come as students mainstream into campus activities or attend other college classes.

Variations on this "supported education" model, as the Center for Psychiatric Rehabilitation calls the Boston University program, are present at the Buffalo Psychiatric Center (the state hospital) with the support of Buffalo State College, Buffalo, New York. Here the young people use the resources of the college to take courses, with support provided from the hospital personnel. Another model of supported education, referred to as a "mobile" model, is the Community Scholar Program at Thresholds, a prominent psychosocial rehabilitation center in Chicago. The supported education model is derived, in part, from the supported employment model, in which a normal work setting (educational setting) is used along with supporting staff and programs to enable the disabled persons to perform in the workaday world. It is expected that gradually the special supporting staff can be lessened and eventually not needed at all (Supported Education, 1990).

It should be kept in mind that many of the programs for transition of disabled youngsters from school to work or higher education are financially supported, in part at least, by special grants of the U.S. Department of Education under provisions of the Education for All Handicapped Children Act of 1975 (P.L. 94-142). As these grants expire, and as the funding of special education services competes with ever limited funding for regular education, it is difficult to know the extent to which these special services will survive. Nevertheless, the mandate for educating the handicapped exists, and hopefully the most successful elements of these demonstration and experimental programs will be built into many educational systems.

Before we examine the educational content, the vocational elements, and the economic issues involved in these programs for transition of psychiatrically handicapped youngsters from school to work, we should look more closely at the characteristics of the youngsters themselves and our understanding of their needs. The reader will learn why I believe that at this time in the development of services the mental health field rather than that of education will have to take the lead in providing for emotionally disturbed and mentally ill youngsters the programs needed for transition to the world of work.

CHAPTER 2

THE ADOLESCENTS

What kinds of children are special programs being developed to aid in their transition to adulthood and the workaday world? A rough sample of mental health and psychiatric services described the youngsters as presenting the following:

Adolescent-onset thought disorders

Anxiety/depression

Attention deficit disorders

Autism

Borderline psychotic diagnosis

Childhood schizophrenia

Developmental handicaps

Eating disorders

Hallucinations

Oppositional behavior

Parent-child conflicts

Parental rejection

Agencies providing social services for children and adolescents reported the children as exhibiting the following:

Abuse

Behavioral/conduct disorders

Delinquency

Depression

Family emotional disturbance

Family poverty

Functional illiteracy

Inability to handle success or failure

Interpersonal deficits

Not being future oriented

No skills for work

Numerous foster placements

Poor peer relationships

Poor self-concept

Possible neurological deficits

School drop out

School failure

Social skills deficits; delayed social and language skills

Substance abuse; chemical dependency

Suicidal acts or ideation; self-destructiveness

Undersocialized quality

Teachers used the following terminology:

Emotionally disturbed

Fire setter

Hyperactive

Language disorder

Learning disability

Liar

Low self-esteem

Physically aggressive

Poor response to authority

Problems with impulse control

Runaway

Steals

Verbally aggressive; verbally abusive

Withdrawal

Of course, for each child only some of the above descriptors were used, but in the final analysis the labels defined youngsters whom the school systems find it hard, difficult, or impossible to absorb into the normal school setting. In the next chapter I shall describe the organization of schooling to try to meet the needs of these youngsters.

ADOLESCENCE

Common to all of these children is that they have entered into that developmental period known as adolescence, widely recognized as a potentially difficult transitional time. Curiously, the concept of adolescence is a product of this century, coined by a social psychologist, G. S. Hall, in 1904 (Hall, 1904). Hall, who is "often referred to as the father of the psychology of adolescence, viewed adolescence as a discontinuous experience—a period that is qualitatively and quantitatively different from childhood and from adulthood." According to deAnda, Hall "labeled the period as one of *sturm und drang.*" His "biogenic approach posited that adolescence was a 'recapitulation' of one of mankind's stages of evolution—a turbulent time for the species and, therefore, for the individual" (deAnda, 1987).

Though many who educate or treat adolescents hold to the *sturm und drang* description, it is important to note that studies of teenagers in relatively "normal" families have increasingly cast doubt upon its applicability except for the most disturbed. As early as 1959, students of adolescent behavior reported that "the foregoing storm and stress picture of adolescence receives little support from detailed information. . .obtained in a study of middle class families of adolescent boys" (Bandura, 1980, p. 23). More recently, a series of studies by Daniel Offer and his associates "have not supported the 'adolescent turmoil' views" (Offer et al., 1988). They state:

> We have found empirically that it is possible for many normal adolescents to integrate their new affective, cognitive, biological, and social experiences and still grow with relatively little disruption. It is clear that adolescence has

> unique features, as does every stage of life. Each stage in life brings new challenges and opportunities. But the changes each stage brings may be relatively easily incorporated into the basic personality structure. (p. 3)

They conclude that "the findings of these empirical studies suggest emphatically that a state of turmoil need no longer be the password of adolescence" (p. 3).

However, Louise Kaplan (1984) is just as emphatic in her disagreement with Offer and his colleagues. She states, "Adolescence is a kind of emotional battleground on which the past and the future contend for mastery over the adult mind that is about to emerge" (p. 14). She questions the adequacy of the studies by Offer and his research associates and the "self-image" questionnaire they developed and used on more than 15 thousand adolescents. She notes that

> the researchers realized that a questionnaire that invited teenagers to confide their secrets by responding to such items as "Dirty jokes are fun sometimes" and "I believe I can tell the real from the fantastic" might be disparaged. In a telephone interview with the [*New York*] *Times* reporter, Dr. Howard [one of the research team] explained: "We were studying the ways kids see themselves; that was our focus. Of course, somebody looking at unconscious conflicts wouldn't do it with a questionnaire. (p. 40)

Dr. Offer and his associates did explain, however, that

> we did find a significant minority of the normative group studied (approximately 15%) describe themselves as de-

pressed, anxious, emotionally empty, or confused. This figure is high and indicates that turmoil and maladaptation are a real part of many teenagers' lives. This subgroup of adolescents includes psychiatric patients, juvenile delinquents, those who deviate radically from their parents' social values, and possibly the specially gifted. Adolescents who experience turmoil most likely grow up in a confusing, emotionally empty, or hostile familial system. But these adolescents were far outnumbered by those who were relatively happy, coped well with their lives, and made a relatively smooth transition to adulthood. (p. 3)

Writing for educators, Adelson (1986) pointed out that

psychological disturbances appearing in adolescence are unlikely to be transient, and are more likely the debut appearance of chronic or continuing disorders. The more severe the symptom picture in adolescence, the more likely it is that later disturbances will be serious or disabling. Strong feelings of resentment, anger, or alienation felt toward the parents will likely continue later in life, though they may be expressed differently. The same may be used for strong feelings of any kind—dependency, for example. (p. 134)

Although all cultures in one way or another have recognized the development of puberty, before the onset of industrialization there is no reference to anything like adolescence. The phenomenon seems to have come into recognition with the changes in the roles of family members and the demands for youngsters to work outside of the family constellation typical of the industrial revolution. Over the years, each succeeding psychological theory has developed its own explanation of adolescence.

DeAnda has divided the theories into psychosexual, psychosocial, and social learning (deAnda, 1987). Her category of psychosexual refers generally to the psychoanalysts. She said:

> According to the psychosexual theorists, two tasks must be accomplished during this stage if psychological maturity is to be attained: (1) detachment from the opposite sex parent as an incestuous love object and (2) establishment of a nonantagonistic, non-dominated relationship with the same sex parent. This process of detachment may result in negativism and hostility toward parents and other authority figures for a time. S. Freud believed that this process is seldom completed ideally. (p. 54)

Anna Freud commented that adolescence:

> is not merely a temporary exaggeration of mechanisms [phallic, pubertal, and climacteric stages] set for all time in childhood but has a pattern peculiar to itself. The frequent extreme asceticism of the teens, for example, often appears to represent a fear of all libidinal impulses, punctuated by an almost orgiastic giving way to them regardless of the taboos peculiar to the individual which will set the pattern of his neurosis in the event that the flare-up of the teens continues. (A. Freud, 1937, p. 152)

Blos modified traditional psychoanalytic theory. He stressed the cultural milieu and social stratum in personality development. Although he saw adolescence as a transitional period recapitulating earlier familial patterns of interaction, "he considered this process to be qualitatively different because of the significant maturation of the ego during the latency period" (deAnda 1987, p. 54). According to deAnda, Blos believed

> The second individuation process that occurs during adolescence requires a "normative regression in the service of development"; that is, only in adolescence is regression an essential and normal process. Though normal, this regression still produces turmoil, volatile behavior, and anxiety that, if it becomes unmanageable, may result in the use of a variety of defense mechanisms such as withdrawal and secrecy, fantasy, temporary compulsive habit formation, compensation, intellectualization, rationalization, projection, and changes in the ego ideal. (Blos, 1941, p. 260; 1979, p. 153)

Ginsburg (1963) put it more simply:

> The younger child yearns to grow up, to be like an adult. The growing girl anticipates menstruation, and her male counterpart practices shaving a nonexistent beard. But with adolescence it is as though such fooling around with being a grownup comes to a halt and the youngster must get down to the business of maturing. He has been evicted from childhood, and the loss of its protection and the vista of adulthood with all its responsibilities seem utterly appalling. As long as he could cling to the privileges of childhood he was not quite so frightened at the prospect of being an adult. But now adolescence forces him to recognize that adulthood is near at hand, and all the successive physical changes serve as constant reminders. As if this weren't

enough, his elders frequently put it into words for him: "You're not a child anymore." (p. 62)

A step apart from the psychosexual theories of instinctual development is what deAnda referred to as the psychosocial element (deAnda, 1987). For example, she said,

> Erikson generalizes beyond the sphere of instinctual development. . . . He points out that the child, now the young adult, must find an identity. This identity is by no means a mere repetition of identification with the father in consequence of a renascent Oedipus complex, or of the rebellion and compromise instituted earlier. It is the accrued experience of his own identity, matched with his perception of his potential meaning for others—as evidenced in the tangible promise of a "career." (Erikson, 1950, p. 228)

The social learning theories are exemplified by the writings of Albert Bandura, Jean Piaget, and Harry Stack Sullivan. In general, though the behavioral and social learning principles that apply in infancy and childhood remain the same, the environment is thought to play a larger part in their utilization. There is "a greater number and variety of models, and an expanded capacity for self-regulated behavior" (deAnda, 1987, p. 55). Bandura and Walters pointed out that they do not believe that research has borne out the claim that adolescence is a sudden or drastic change from childhood. They believe, instead, that the pattern is one of socialization toward independence by means of a gradual change in the conditions of reinforcement (Bandura & Walters, 1963).

Piaget and his colleagues looked upon the changes in thinking from childhood to adolescence as exemplifying a progression from concrete to formal, as the product of individual "spontaneous and endogenous factors" that stimulate intellectual growth. They allow the adolescent to "analyze his own thinking and construct theories" (Piaget & Inhelder, 1958). It is the belief of the social learning theorists that moral development takes place in adolescence. It is during this period that capacity for empathy develops.

> As a result of his or her cognitive development, the adolescent begins to conceptualize others not only as distinct but to project the self into another's experiences beyond the immediate concrete situation and, therefore to respond with empathetic distress and a more reciprocal feeling of concern for the victim. . . . In social learning theory, moral values, judgements, and behaviors are viewed as being dependent on a variety of environmental factors, such as the long and short-term consequences, the setting, the type of act, and the characteristics of the victim. (deAnda, 1987, p. 55)

> (See also Bandura, 1977; Rosenthal & Zimmerman, 1978; and Hoffman, 1980.)

CAREER CHOICE

The adolescent years are ones in which decisions are made as to future work life. As Ginsburg points out, "With few exceptions, this too is a final choice; once they have decided on a field of work, few people have the opportunity to change it. Where education and training are basically involved, few can afford the luxury of reeducation and retraining. Even when expense is not a consideration, a choice commits one to a whole way of life, often to a geographical location, and it is rarely that one can undo such decisions once they have been made" (Ginsburg, 1963, p. 64). Certainly this is true for leaving school and choosing a vocational trade or training or continuing on to higher education. Although those choosing the latter have a little more time in deciding which career they will finally enter, most adolescents do believe, and are often pressured by their advisers to believe, they must quickly make this choice. Munroe points out, "Furthermore, the adolescent is expected by his culture to assume adulthood, in a manner definitely formalized by many cultures, implicit in all. One of the most obvious facts about adolescents is that they press urgently toward the cultural image of adulthood with much underlying anxiety and reversion to earlier attitudes" (Munroe, 1955, p. 411).

Years ago, Gellman coined the term "work personality" to describe the attributes expected of the successful working man or woman (Gellman et al., 1955). Building on this, Neff pointed out that what he called "occupational identity" is developed during the process of formal education. "It is the school performance itself which becomes the crucial determinant of his later occupational role. The school drop-out is mostly confined to unskilled, common labor, since almost any kind of skilled work requires some mastery of the high school subjects. In general, although there is far from a perfect correlation, the more skilled, rewarding, and prestigious an occupation is, the more formal education it requires" (Neff,

1968, p. 3).

The 1950s and 1960s were periods in which much was made of the "identity crisis" in contemporary society (see Erikson, 1950, 1963; Wheelis, 1953; Fromm, 1948, 1955). In the psychoanalytic theory predominant at the time the development of a vocational identity was strongly tied to the adolescent's relationship to his or her father. Pearson commented, "The explanation I have found... does not explain why so many adolescents cannot select a vocation while still in high school; for, obviously, all of them have not been separated from their fathers. However, they may all have had an unconscious dread of growing up lest they die. . . . The fact remains that achieving a personal identity through vocation seems to be attained later and to a lessened degree than it used to be" (Pearson, 1958, pp. 149-150). This complaint, that the actual assumption of adult duties and responsibilities seems to be increasingly delayed, is one repeated through the years. What is specifically referred to, of course, is the acquisition of a job, of employment, in our culture the embodiment of the adult role. Pearson noted in the 1950s:

> Although the American community and educational systems permit the adolescent a certain number of trial and error opportunities of learning to take responsibility, they place many restrictions in his way. . . . The adolescent. . . profits by having some kind of gainful work; but it should be work chosen by himself and of a regular kind. . . . The community and educational systems in other ways place fixed limits on the adolescent's opportunities to earn money. Child labor laws prevent his exploitation. . . and the school law says a child must remain in school until he is sixteen or older. These restrictions are generally wise. . . . The restrictions, however, do interfere with certain opportunities for the adolescent to learn to take responsibility. For

> instance, adolescents under sixteen—particularly boys—
> would profit greatly from being able to earn money by
> working—and not by work made in the family. . . . He feels
> entirely different if, without any urging from his parents, he
> takes it upon himself to mow his neighbor's lawn for a set
> price. (Pearson, 1958, pp. 99-100)

These are exactly the sentiments expressed today, except that they now apply to girls as well as to boys. The observation that the gap is ever widening between adolescent years and the assumption of adulthood is related both to the greater demands of educational preparation for the workaday world and to the changing character of jobs themselves. I shall have more to say on these points in a later chapter.

ADOLESCENT TROUBLES

Adolescence, then, is a period in which a great many things are happening to the child, from psychosexual development to changes in environmental expectations. That there is a potential for things to go wrong in even the most "normal" situations almost goes without saying. In discussing the prolongation of adolescent status, the psychoanalyst Pearson comments that:

> the great body of information an adolescent must master is
> too much for him to learn until long after biological,
> developmental, and chronological maturity has been
> reached. This discrepancy cannot help but be reflected in
> his emotional life. It does not help him attain emotional
> stability or develop a sense of responsibility, for it means
> either that his rebellion against dependence on the family is
> more severe than it need be, or that he must erect very rigid
> intrapsychic defenses against his rebellious feelings.
> (Pearson, 1958, p. 152).

Later on Pearson points out:

> The more society prolongs adolescence. . . the more it
> encourages the passive receptive wishes present in all
> people. The child or adolescent in whom these wishes are
> encouraged has two courses open to him: he may remain
> governed by his passive receptive desires and demand that
> his environment continue to gratify him; or he may sud-
> denly decide, perhaps in latency, perhaps not until late
> adolescence, that he consciously does not like these char-
> acteristics in himself, possibly because he finds they cannot
> be gratified. He therefore represses them into his uncon-
> scious, and develops a reaction formation against them in
> his conscious feelings, attitudes and behavior. The indi-
> vidual who remains passive cannot be a useful member of
> society. The individual who consciously decides he does
> not want to be passive may become delinquent, or may
> develop serious disturbances in the function of one or more
> important organs in his body. He is unable to tolerate the
> stresses of his life because he is constantly laboring under
> the extra tension imposed by the intrapsychic conflict
> between his unconscious passive receptive desires and his
> reaction formations against them. (Pearson, 1958, p. 157)

Pearson concludes, "We seem to expect that the adolescent
will adjust himself to a situation which the man or woman of
thirty would instantly repudiate." He answers the question
"What can be done to help the adolescent during these difficult
years?" as follows: "About all that can be said is that the
adolescent has to learn to adapt himself to the culture and the
social organization in which he lives; and if this adaptation is
difficult, and if the culture gives him little help, he still has to
learn to adjust himself to it" (Pearson, 1958, p. 171). Ginsburg
comes to a similar conclusion, "After all my years of experi-

ence, in fact, I know of nothing that so completely defied any generalized prescription as adolescence. I believe this is so because its conditioning begins in the cradle. I often feel that in the end the only solace for adolescent and adult alike is the recognition that this too passes" (Ginsburg, 1963, p. 68).

To provide a basis for treatment of disturbed or deviant adolescents, the sociologist Talcott Parsons formulated the concept of a *youth culture*. This has now become well incorporated into our language. Parsons (1950, pp. 378-379) summarized the principal characteristics of youth culture as follows:

1. Compulsive independence of and antagonism to adult expectations and authority. This involves recalcitrance to adult standards of responsibility and, in extreme instances, treating the conformist—who, for instance takes school work seriously—as a "sissy" who should be excluded from peer group participation.

2. Compulsive conformity within the peer group of agemates. . . . Related to this is an intense fear of being excluded, a corresponding competitiveness for acceptance by the "right" groups, and a ruthless rejection of those who don't make the grade.

3. Romanticism: an unrealistic idealization of emotionally significant objects. There is a general tendency to see the world in sharply black and white terms; identification with one's gang or team, or school tends to be very intense and involves highly immature disparagement of other groups.

If this is a description of the average adolescent behavior, it is clear how difficult it must be to deal with youngsters who deviate even more markedly from the general youth culture.

A really disturbed adolescent can create havoc in a household. The hostility of such a youngster may provoke the adults in his environment from tolerance and patient forbearance to a retaliatory show of strength and often to overt hostility. And this establishes a vicious cycle that ultimately involves the child, his brothers and sisters, parents, grandparents, friends, teachers—in short, everyone with whom he is in contact—in a frenzy of trying to deal adequately with the consequences of his behavior. Such situations are beyond easy understanding and eventually require some kind of treatment. (Ginsburg, 1963, p. 68)

MENTAL ILLNESS

As must be clear by now, there is a very wide array of behaviors to which a classification of mental illness or emotional disturbance may be ascribed. A great many acts of the adolescent that differ from the expected norms of childhood (or that might even be explained in a younger person as "childishness") or of adulthood could be denoted psychological aberrations. In fact, a review of the studies of prevalence of childhood psychopathology in the general population concludes that "the prevalence of clinical maladjustment in the U.S. is probably no lower than 11.8 percent" (Gould et al., 1981, p. 476). A recent study of nearly 800 children, aged 7 to 11, who were treated at a health maintenance organization in Pittsburgh, identified 22% as having had a psychiatric problem at some point in the previous year (Goleman, 1989). Furthermore, even when youngsters were identified as "disturbed," 50% of them were not recognized as needing psychiatric help (Offer et al., 1986).

How then are diagnoses of mental illness arrived at? In the years before the advent of child guidance clinics in the late 1920s and 1930s, children were categorized as either "dependent" or "delinquent." The concept that divergent behavior might result from mental illness did not gain acceptance to any great extent until after World War II. The institutional movement was in sway, and most children with "behavior and personality problems" were remanded or committed to institutions for dependent and neglected children or to training schools. In later years, many of these institutions became "residential treatment centers" as the children and adolescents began to be diagnosed as mentally ill (Petr & Spano, 1990). Outpatient treatment was provided through child guidance clinics, which in more recent years have been folded into the children's services of community mental health centers.

To an ever-increasing extent the classification of "mental illness," or as preferred by educational authorities, "emotional disturbance," is made in accord with the DSM-III-R (American Psychiatric Association, 1987, p. 27-95). There, the major "disorders first evident in infancy, childhood, or adolescence" are listed as developmental disorders (including mental retardation), disruptive behavior disorders (including attention deficit hyperactivity disorder, conduct disorder, oppositional defiant disorder), anxiety disorders of childhood or adolescence, eating disorders (including anorexia nervosa, bulimia nervosa), gender identity disorders, tic disorders, elimination disorders, and an assortment of less frequent disorders. In addition, of course, are the major psychiatric disturbances (organic, psychoactive, schizophrenia, mood disorders, personality disorders, and so on) that are more frequently found in adults.

Although the major psychoses have been identified as

being present at times in childhood, their greatest incidence occurs in late adolescence or young adulthood. For the schizophrenics, the first serious manifestations appear when most public schooling has been completed, and the mood disorders (depressive and bipolar disorders) don't usually show up until the twenties or thirties. When these serious ailments occur in childhood or early adolescence the youngster is most likely to be hospitalized or in other residential treatment than to remain in school. Increasingly frequent is the incarceration in jail or penitentiary of older mentally ill adolescents whose behavior is threatening or damaging to other persons or to property.

Individuals with the diagnosis of personality disorder are more likely to be adults than adolescents, for the substantiation of personality disorder requires confirmation of its elements over a period of time. In childhood, the manifestations of personality and conduct disorders are for the most part indistinguishable according to the classifications of DSM-III-R.

By far the most frequent emotional disorders reported for school children are in the conduct disorder groupings. A large-scale longitudinal study of children identified as seriously emotionally disturbed by the public mental health system or the public educational system (Friedman et al., 1988, p. 13) concluded that conduct disorder was the most prevalent diagnosis obtained. "It occurs nearly as often as a combined disorder with emotional problems as it does as a single diagnosis; it tends to co-occur with anxiety and depression—characteristics typically not viewed as co-existing with this disorder." It should be kept in mind that there is no magic in diagnostic classifications. Their value is in designing treatment approaches, but in the context of developing programs of transition from school to work their main value is in attesting to the presence of disability. Wood and Lakin (1982) described a study that found "that public school programs had high percentages of children with 'behavior problems' (conduct disorders), while residential schools had higher percentages of children with 'personality disorders' and private day schools higher percentages of students labeled 'psychotic.' His findings suggest that both problem behavior, and the descriptors used to label it may vary as a function of the vocabulary preferred by the professionals dominant in a given setting" (p. 9). It should be kept in mind that a "misbehaving" child is not eligible for the special education services guaranteed by federal and state laws and regulations; a child diagnosed with a conduct disorder or learning disablement or the like is a disabled youngster under the laws.

DSM-III-R describes conduct disorder as "a persistent pattern of conduct in which the basic rights of others and major age-appropriate societal norms or rules are violated. The behavior pattern typically is present in the home, at school, with peers, and in the community. The conduct problems are more serious than those seen in Oppositional Defiant Disorder" (American Psychiatric Association, 1987, pp. 53-55). The diagnostic criteria include:

A. A disturbance of conduct lasting at least six months, during which at least three of the following have been present:
1. has stolen without confrontation of a victim on more than one occasion (including forgery)
2. has run away from home overnight at least twice while living in parental or parental surrogate home (or once without returning)
3. often lies (other than to avoid physical or sexual abuse)
4. has deliberately engaged in fire-setting
5. is often truant from school . . .

    6. has broken into someone else's house, building or car

    7. has deliberately destroyed others' property (other than by fire-setting)

    8. has been physically cruel to animals

    9. has forced someone into sexual activity with him or her

  10. has used a weapon in more than one fight

  11. often initiates physical fights

  12. has stolen with confrontation of a victim (e.g., mugging, purse-snatching, extortion, armed robbery)

  13. has been physically cruel to people

> NOTE: The above items are listed in descending order of discriminating power based on data from a national field trial of the DSM-III-R criteria for Disruptive Behavior Disorders.

B. If 18 or older, does not meet criteria for Antisocial Personality Disorder.

The explanation given in DSM-III-R of the consideration of age in the diagnosis of conduct disorder is as follows:

> Personality *traits* are enduring patterns of perceiving, relating to, and thinking about the environment and oneself, and are exhibited in a wide range of important social and personal contexts. It is only when *personality traits* are inflexible and maladaptive and cause either significant functional impairment or subjective distress that they constitute *Personality Disorders*. The manifestations of Personality Disorders are often recognizable by adolescence or earlier and continue throughout most of adult life, though they often become less obvious in middle or old age.... The diagnosis of Conduct Disorder, rather than Antisocial Personality Disorder, should be made if the person is under 18, since studies have indicated that many children with prominent antisocial behavior do not continue to exhibit antisocial behavior in adulthood. (American Psychiatric Associa-

tion, 1987, pp. 335-336)

In a comprehensive review of our knowledge about conduct disorders, Quay (1986) describes two patterns, undersocialized and socialized, as:

> the most prevalent form of childhood and adolescent disorder, with a preponderance of males at a ratio of at least three to one. The correlates of the undersocialized pattern include deficient verbal mediational skills, poor social skills, persistent failure in social intervention programs, and a generally poorer prognosis for successful adult living than . . . any other disorder except psychosis. While environmental factors play a major etiological role . . . recent research has implicated psychophysiological and biochemical factors.
>
> The socialized form is not associated with cognitive deficits or demonstrably poor social relations. Neither are there any intimations of a biological component in its etiology. While childhood behavior related to this pattern is clearly related to delinquency in adolescence, adjustment in adult life appears to be superior to that of the undersocialized form.
>
> The social cost of the conduct disorders is high. . . . Clearly, no other disorder of childhood and adolescence is so widespread and disruptive of the lives of those who suffer it and of the lives of others, and thus it deserved continued research investigation. (p. 64)

Much is being studied and written about the "borderline syndrome" as a serious disorder of young people. These complex disturbances, frequently aggravated by alcohol and drug addictions, are more common to older adolescents and young adults. The concept of borderline syndrome, as I recall

it, had its origin in the attempts of the child guidance movement nearly half a century ago to classify and treat a group of
adolescents who did not quite fit a diagnosis of schizophrenia
(amid questions about its applicability to children) and whose
behavior was not sufficiently delinquent to call for admission
to a mental hospital or "training school." The DSM-III-R
manual describes the criteria for borderline personality disorder as:

> A pervasive pattern of instability of mood, interpersonal
> relationships, and self-image, beginning by early adult-
> hood and present in a variety of contexts, as indicated by at
> least five of the following:
>
> 1. a pattern of unstable and intense interpersonal rela-
>   tionships characterized by alternating between ex-
>   tremes of overidealization and devaluation
> 2. impulsiveness in at least two areas that are potentially
>   self-damaging, e.g., spending, sex, substance use,
>   shoplifting, reckless driving, binge eating
> 3. affective instability: marked shifts from baseline mood
>   to depression, irritability, or anxiety, usually lasting a
>   few hours and only rarely more than a few days
> 4. inappropriate, intense anger or lack of control of
>   anger, e.g., frequent displays of temper, constant
>   anger, recurrent physical fights
> 5. recurrent suicidal threats, gestures, or behavior, or
>   self-mutilating behavior
> 6. marked and persistent identity disturbance mani-
>   fested by uncertainty about at least two of the follow-
>   ing: self-image, sexual orientation, long-term goals
>   or career choice, type of friends desired, preferred
>   values
> 7. chronic feelings of emptiness or boredom

8. frantic efforts to avoid real or imagined abandon-
ment. (DSM-III-R, 1987, pp. 346-347)

In general use, the term "borderline syndrome" has given way
to the designation "young adult chronic patient." This latter
term had its origin in attempts to identify the increasing
numbers of younger patients who were being admitted to
public mental hospitals in the United States and in Europe in
the late 1960s and early 1970s. With the emphasis upon early
discharge from the hospital, deinstitutionalization, and community mental health care, these young folk who in an earlier
period would have been expected to spend most of their lives
in the hospital were now out in the community requiring
treatment. A study of cohorts of these patients between 1977
and 1982 showed that while age, ethnicity, sex, and diagnostic
groupings did not change, the later group exhibited less
education, more unemployment, and an increase in the abuse
of drugs (Gralnick et al., 1986). In comparison of the patients
in the age range 16 through 25 to those in the range 26 through
35, the younger patients were found to have had earlier onset
of illness, were more likely to have been diagnosed as schizophrenic, had unstable life-styles before admission to the
hospital, had more intellectual impairment, had greater unemployment, stayed in the hospital longer, and were less likely to
be discharged improved. Those in the older group were more
likely to be diagnosed as substance abusers.

In any discussion of serious mental illness, it must be kept
in mind that genetic influences and organic involvements play
some significant part in their incidence. This is particularly
true when a major psychosis is present for one or more of the
child's parents.

Compared to a risk of one to two percent in the general
population, children of one schizophrenic parent have a

lifetime risk of roughly 12 percent, while children of two
schizophrenic parents have the exceptionally high risk of
35 to 46 percent. . . . Particularly noteworthy, however, is
the finding. . . that teachers' reports of poor affective
control (easily upset, affect persists when excited, disturbs
class by unusual behavior, presents disciplinary problems)
and difficulty making friends discriminated adolescent
children of schizophrenic parents who subsequently had
schizophrenic episodes from high-risk children with more
healthy adult outcomes. (Asarnow, 1988, p. 1613)

LEARNING DISABILITY

As I pointed out in Chapter 1, among the mental illnesses
listed in DSM-III-R is a developmental disorder called attention deficit hyperactivity disorder, or ADHD (American Psychiatric Association, 1987). The criteria distinctions between
attention deficit disorder and conduct disorder are by no
means clear cut: "Since it is clear that poor academic performance is associated with Attention Deficit Disorder (where it
is also clear that the disorder antedates the academic problems), special care must be taken not to confound these two
groups, as is often the case" (Quay, 1986, p. 40; see also
Margalit, 1989). As Links has shown in his review of community surveys of psychiatric disorders, "Behavioral symptoms,
characteristic of children attending mental health facilities,
are exceedingly common in the general population . . . the
method of defining and measuring deviance has been found to
effect greatly the prevalence estimates obtained" (Links,
1983, p. 544; see also McKinney, 1989).

Teachers have recognized for many years that some children have great difficulty in organizing and utilizing perceptual and conceptual information. These are the children who seem to persist in not understanding directions, in being unable to copy lines and diagrams, in not being able to read clearly, and who in other ways fail to make the connections between what they hear and see and what they produce in school, in spite of evidence that they have normal or above normal intelligence. Psychologists began to identify these children in the 1960s as suffering from "learning disabilities" (Eaves, 1982, p. 463). These specific difficulties, along with concomitant problems of attention, seemed to many educators and developmental psychologists to constitute a "syndrome," which they called "learning disability." Many attempts have been made to ascribe a common etiology to the syndrome without success. For a time the blame was attributed to brain abnormalities, "minimal brain damage" (MBD); then "minimal cerebral dysfunction" became popular, and "psychoneurological learning disability," but examinations of the brain and neurological tests were not revealing. Nevertheless, a number of educational and psychological tests (scales) could be devised to distinguish these children from normal youngsters, and the classification "learning disabled" has become an accepted category as a handicapping condition (Acters Scale, 1984). Though possible causes range from brain injury to emotional disturbances and environmental conditions, and though the variety of behaviors exhibited is quite great, the tendency is still to speak of learning disability as a single entity. As a leading educator put it, "The learning disorder is a specific syndrome. It is characterized by a disruption in the processing of information within the central nervous system. It arises from a number of etiological situations. It is most prominently observed in learning situations since a major aspect of learning is organization of material. As such, it is of particular significance to education" (Kephart, 1968, p. 14; see also Johnston, 1987).

The designation of learning disability, then, is not strictly medical. Actually, in the process of determining its presence in deciding eligibility for special education benefits (described in the next chapter), information can be provided not only from the doctor and the teacher but from the parents as well. However, Achenbach and his associates (1987) have found that correlations of reports of behavior of adolescents as between any two reporters of different disciplines (e.g., parent and teacher, teacher and doctor) is very low, in the .20 to .40 range. Correlations between like disciplines (doctor/doctor, parent/parent, teacher/teacher) reach .60 and above, quite respectable heights for social science studies. This is not necessarily true, however, when the reports cover different environmental situations. I recall psychiatric opinion in a residential treatment center that a child who was behaving irrationally and wildly was diagnosed as schizophrenic and sent to Bellevue Hospital psychiatric unit for crisis care. The child's behavior at Bellevue, a much stricter, controlled environment, was so normal that the doctors there insisted there was no psychosis. On the child's return to the center the symptoms flared up again. The moral is, don't trust one report or the application of one set of scales.

The conclusion one reaches is that there is great flexibility in deciding a classification of disability in behavior disorders. It becomes understandable that in many cases a designation of "learning disability" would be preferred over the more stigmatizing "emotional disturbance" or "mental illness." As Eaves (1982, p. 463) questioned,

The conceptualization of learning disabilities as a classification among handicapping conditions was introduced by Sam Kirk in 1963. Twelve years later 260,000
children were being served under that rubric. On the
other hand, the conceptualization and treatment of emotional disturbance among children began at least as far
back as the 1700s. Yet in 1975 only 255,000 youngsters
were served under that label. This figure represents less
than one in five of the emotionally disturbed children
estimated to live in the United States. How is it possible
that so few emotionally disturbed children are being
served?

Eaves answers his own question validly, I believe: "The
chief answer probably lies in the fact that most children
diagnosed as emotionally disturbed exhibit behavior that
engenders hostility rather than sympathy. Consequently,
there has never been a ground-swell of support for school
programs designed to serve these youth." He further points
out the difficulty in defining emotional disturbance, particularly in making a distinction between social maladjustment (which does not make children eligible for special
education services) and emotional disturbance (which does).

MENTAL ILLNESS VS. EMOTIONAL DISTURBANCE

For the most part, I have used the terms "mentally ill" and
"emotionally disturbed" interchangeably. But they are not
really synonymous. My friends among the special educa-

tors would heartily agree. Emotional disturbance is not a scientific or medical diagnosis. It is a popularly used term applied to a wide range of psychological disturbances, from psychic upsets to nervous breakdowns to misbehaviors. This label carries little of the fright and stigma attached to mental illness, where there is the connotation that patients may be a danger to themselves or others. Unless there is a formal psychiatric diagnosis, if the behavior of a youngster precludes calling the problem a learning disability, teachers and parents and others are disposed to assign the label of emotional disturbance rather than mental illness or mental disorder. "The child is upset, not crazy," they would insist.

I am very sympathetic to avoiding when possible the label of mental illness, especially for children or adolescents. I do believe that there can be alleviation and sometimes cure of psychiatric illnesses, and labels on young people have a way of following them throughout their lives. Nevertheless, medical determination of conduct disorder or other psychiatric disablement increasingly qualifies children for special education services, and the symptoms that a psychiatrist might diagnose as a DSM-III-R item frequently are called an emotional disturbance by the teacher.

A concomitant issue, part of the stigma attached to mental illness, is the unwillingness of a parent, particularly a mother, to support such a diagnosis for the child because there is still a great tendency to lay the blame for the child's behavior on the mother. I recall with poignant hindsight how absolute was our professional opinion in child guidance clinic days in holding the mother responsible for the mental illness of her progeny. Our case reports were full of terrible and damaging mothers, their lack of nurturant behavior, their failure to "bond" with their infants, as animal studies, particularly of ducks, had shown was necessary for wholesome growth. It is unfortunate, as Caplan and Hall-McCorquodale have reported (1983), that mother-blaming is still rife in the major clinical journals. From here on I shall use the term "emotionally disturbed" in deference to the more usual use in educational circles.

In the next chapter I turn attention to schools and education available for these children who are identified as mentally ill or emotionally disturbed, or often as learning disabled, particularly as the federal education laws have established that they qualify for services as "handicapped children."

CHAPTER 3

SCHOOLS AND EDUCATION

Of all the social institutions involved in the lives of adolescents, probably none is as confusing and often confounding to mental health professionals as the school system. This is so even though for many years there has been cooperation between child guidance workers and school systems and most school systems employ social workers and psychologists, and in some instances psychiatrists, to provide mental health services to troubled children.

In the education of children who have disabilities ("handicaps" in the terminology of the educational system), the past 20 years have brought a mushrooming of new laws and regulations, methods, and practices. Although special education has been a part of public education for most of this century, it really developed nationally only in the last few decades. "By 1967 a large majority of school systems in the United States provided some type of special education services and well over a million children and young people were being served by such programs" (Gearheart, 1967, p. 3).

However, special education in the public schools was then either special schooling for the blind or deaf or "home teaching" for children who were too physically disabled to travel to and from school or who were physically ill and needed help to keep up with schoolwork until they were well enough to return to regular classes. Not every school system made provisions for such home teachers, and those that did had them in limited supply. For the most part, little thought or attention was given in educational planning to the plight of youngsters whose mental or physical handicaps interfered with or precluded their attendance in public school classes.

SPECIAL EDUCATION AS A RIGHT

The first federal commitment to education for the handicapped came with the launching of the first sputnik by the Soviet Union. This produced motivation for the National Defense Education Act of 1958 (P.L. 85-864), which carried the suggestion that supplemental services ought to be made available so that handicapped children could also be educated within the public educational system (Corthell & VanBoskirk, 1984).

In 1963 Congress enacted P.L. 88-164, creating a Division of Handicapped Children and Youth in the Department of Health, Education and Welfare. In 1965, Title I of the Elementary and Secondary Education Act (P.L. 89-10) established a multimillion- dollar program of aid to the states for local school districts having children from low-income families who were considered "educationally disadvantaged." At that time Congress defined "educationally disadvantaged" to include handicapped youngsters. Later in the year Congress amended Title I to provide specific grants to state agencies operating or supporting schools for handicapped children (ESEA, 1965). Later, grants were made under Title I to local educational agencies, first to assist children who were formerly enrolled in state schools and then to be available to all public local educational agencies serving the "educationally deprived." The term "handicapped children" was defined to include youngsters who were hard of hearing, deaf, speech impaired, visually handicapped, deaf-blind, orthopedically disabled or with other health impairment, mentally retarded, seriously emotionally disturbed, or with a specific learning disability.

The Education of the Handicapped Act of 1970 (P.L. 91-230) codified into a single law much of the special education legislation that had preceded it, and set the stage for the discussions and formulations that led to the current all-encompassing federal law popularly referred to as the Education for All Handicapped Children Act (P.L. 94-142). Four other pieces of legislation played roles in extending the rights of handicapped people to receive educational services. These were the Higher Education Amendments of 1972 (P.L. 91-230), which provided specific additional federal support for college and university education of the handicapped; the Economic Opportunity Act Amendments of 1972 (P.L. 92-242), which reserved 10% of the places in the Headstart Program for handicapped preschoolers; Title II of the Education Act Amendments of 1976, directed at vocational education; and the Rehabilitation Act of 1973, with its amendments (P.L. 93-112, P.L. 93-516, and P.L. 95-602). These "have all been looked upon as providing a *Bill of Rights* for persons with disabilities and in holding the promise for the provision of meaningful services and access to public and private institutions" (Corthell & VanBoskirk, 1984, p. 13).

Although these legislative acts reflected a slowly gathering ferment in American society for increasing services to our more disadvantaged and disabled population, it was not until Congress enacted P.L. 94-142, the Education for All Handicapped Children Act, that special education in the public schools took the form it now has. This act "is a primary source of Federal aid to state and local school systems for instructional and support services to handicapped children. The centerpiece of the Act is a state grant-in-aid program, authorized under Part B, which requires participating states to furnish all handicapped children with a free, appropriate public education in the least restrictive setting" (U.S. Department of Education, 1980, p. 5).

There are six parts to the Act. Part A establishes a Bureau of Education for the Handicapped, now located in the Office of the Assistant Secretary for Special Education and Rehabilitative Services, and defines terms and the primary aim of the Act, which is "to assure that all handicapped children have available to them a free appropriate public education which emphasizes special education and related services designed to meet their unique needs" (pp. 5-6). Part B authorizes formula grants to the states to cover a percentage of the costs of providing a "free appropriate public education" to all handicapped children in participating educational systems. These funds are allocated among the states on the basis of a statutory formula that takes into account the relative numbers of handicapped children in the state multiplied by the average per pupil expenditure of all children in public elementary and secondary schools in the country. Part B also includes a separate allotment to encourage the provision of special education to preschool handicapped children.

Part C of P.L. 94-142 provides for regional resource centers to offer advice and technical assistance to educators to improve instructional services for handicapped children. It also includes project grants for establishing centers and services for deaf-blind children; experimental demonstrations in early childhood education for handicapped children; innovative programs for severely handicapped children; regional programs of vocational-technical, postsecondary, or adult education for handicapped persons; and training for educators and other personnel serving handicapped children.

Grants to provide for disseminating information to parents of handicapped children and to assist in recruiting potential teachers were authorized in Part D. Research and demonstration project grants were included in Part E, and grants for developing instructional media and captioned films for the handicapped were provided in Part F (P.L. 94-142).

Special education is defined in the Education for All Handicapped Children Act as "specially designed instruction, at no cost to parents or guardians, to meet the unique needs of a handicapped child, including classroom instruction, instruction in physical education, home instruction, and instruction in hospitals and institutions" (Sect. 1401 [a] [16]). The act covers children of ages 3 to 21 except for a few states that exclude preschoolers and those in the age range 18 to 21. The major provisions of the law that concern us here are those dealing with the following aspects:

Least restrictive environment

Free appropriate public education

Individualized educational program

Due process procedures

Corthell and VanBoskirk (1984, p. 18) list several principles embodied in P.L. 94-142. These are:

1. States must make publicly supported appropriate education available to all handicapped children of ages 3 through 18 by September 1978, and to all handicapped children ages 3 through 21 by 1979.
2. Local and state education agencies must utilize an Individualized Education Program (IEP) in determining the educational program for each handicapped youngster.
3. Handicapped and nonhandicapped children are to be educated together to the maximum extent appropriate to providing quality education. This is to be the "least restrictive environment" for the handicapped children.
4. Education agencies are to seek, locate, and identify handicapped children to determine whether their educational needs are being met.
5. Priority is to be given to providing education for those handicapped children receiving no education at all, then to the most severely handicapped in each disability category.
6. Diagnostic tests are not to be culturally or racially discriminatory.
7. Each state must have an advisory panel including handicapped persons and parents or guardians of handicapped children.

In considering the effect of this legislation upon services to handicapped children, it is important to keep in mind certain characteristics of P.L. 94-142. The law sets the primary responsibility for ensuring that educational services are actually provided with each state department of education. The state departments, in addition, have the responsibilities of administering the program in their states, doing statewide planning, developing guidelines and regulations, disbursing federal and state funds to the local educational agencies (LEAs), and monitoring that the LEAs follow the state and federal laws. The federal law authorized a sizable amount of funding to the states for these purposes. In the 1990 federal fiscal year, some 4.2 billion dollars was obligated for the purposes of education of handicapped children (World Almanac, 1991, p. 209). In contrast to the more usual practice in congressional legislation, P.L. 94-142 carries no expiration date. The availability of federal funding, in the face of awakened interest on the part of parents and the general citizenry in demanding services for handicapped children, was a great stimulant for the development of special education in all of the states and local school districts.

THE INDIVIDUALIZED EDUCATIONAL PROGRAM

The linchpin of the processes set up by P.L. 94-142 is the Individualized Education Program (IEP). The IEP constitutes the first step in classifying youngsters as handicapped, in evaluating their educational needs, in developing a plan of education, and in placing them in the proper school setting. The specific components of the IEP, as defined in the federal regulations, are listed below.

A. A statement of the child's present levels of educational performance;

B. A statement of the annual goals, including short-term instructional objectives;

C. A statement of the specific educational services to be

provided to the child, and the extent to which the child will be able to participate in the regular educational program;

D. The projected date for the initiation of services and anticipated duration of services; and

E. Appropriate objective criteria and evaluation procedures, and a schedule for determining, on at least an annual basis, whether the short-term instructional objectives are being achieved. (National Association of State Boards of Education, 1979, p. 11)

This information is to result in "a written statement for each handicapped child developed in any meeting by a representative of the local education agency or an intermediate educational unit who shall be qualified to provide, or supervise the provision of, specially designed instruction to meet the unique needs of handicapped children, the teacher, the parents or guardian of such child, and whenever appropriate, such child" (p. 11). Each state, if it did not already have legal or regulatory provisions for interdisciplinary committees to classify and evaluate handicapped children, changed its education laws to conform with P.L. 94-142. At the local school district level, IEP committees (sometimes called Committees on Special Education or Committees on the Handicapped) set about developing the written program plans called for by the federal law.

In its simplest form, such as in New York State (New York State Education Law, 1979), the committees responsible for the IEP are required to be composed of the following:

A representative of the local education agency who is qualified to provide or supervise the provision of special education

The teacher or teachers of the child

The parents or guardian

The child, whenever appropriate

Other states make provision for an expanded attendance at IEP committee meetings. Massachusetts, for example, provides in its regulations for the implementation of its Special Education Law (Rittenhouse, 1980) for the following members of its IEP committees:

1. Director of special education—chairperson
2. Registered nurse or social worker or counselor with M.A. degree
3. Psychologist
4. Teacher most familiar with the child
5. Physician or designee
6. Local school administrator
7. Parent of the child
8. Upcoming teacher
9. Primary person who will be assisting the teacher in implementing the program
10. Outside person working with the child at parent's request
11. Vocational-educational person for adolescents of ages 16 through 21
12. Additional specialists who must be approved by the parents.

Much more common, however, is the minimal makeup of the South Carolina special education committees, which include "the psychologist, a person obtaining the child's social history, a person presenting the child's medical records, and a member of the district's administrative staff. Additional persons may include the person initiating the referral, the special teacher who may receive the pupil, guidance specialists, etc. The parent must be invited to the staffing" (Evans, 1979, p. 10).

CLASSIFICATION

The special education committee that has the responsibility of developing the IEP first must determine that the child meets the state and federal definitions of a handicapped child. Public Law 94-142 Sect. 1401 (a)(10) defines handicapped as "... mentally retarded, hard of hearing, deaf, orthopedically impaired, other health impaired, speech impaired, visually handicapped, seriously emotionally disturbed, or children with specific learning disabilities who, by reason thereof, require special education and related services." Each state has written the same list or a varied version of it into its education laws and regulations. In addition, the state regulations describe in greater detail what is meant by each handicapped status. For example, the West Virginia Department of Education (Taylor, 1978) describes a behavioral disordered child as:

> an individual . . . whose manifest behavior has a deleterious effect on his personal or educational development and/or the personal or educational development of others. Nega-

tive effects may vary considerably from one child to another in terms of severity and prognosis. These behavior(s) may appear separately or in combination and may be exhibited in the form of:

1. Acting-out behavior (hitting, aggressiveness, overactive, disrespect of authority, disruptive behaviors, etc.);
2. Withdrawing behaviors (absence of speech, thumbsucking, restricted behaviors, head-banging, etc.);
3. Defensive behaviors (lying, cheating, avoiding tasks, etc.);
4. Disorganized behaviors (autistic behavior, out of touch with reality, etc.) (p. 19)

It is supportive of my contention that there is frequent overlap in definition that in listing what it calls "some common characteristics of exceptionalities" Taylor's report says of behavioral disorders that they "may exhibit some characteristics found under learning disabilities" (p. 23).

EVALUATION FOR PLACEMENT

The data to be considered in arriving at a plan for educational placement of the handicapped youngster are spelled out in the education regulations in each state. In South Carolina, for example, the placement decision must be based upon intelligence test results plus "information from other sources, e.g., teacher recommendations, physical conditions, social and cultural background, and adaptive behavior" (Evans, 1979, p. 8). In operation, the intelligence measure must be the Wechsler

Intelligence Scale for Children—Revised (WISC-R) or Stanford-Binet Intelligence Scales (by far the most popular tests used); the identification of a qualifying "severe discrepancy between achievement and intellectual ability" would be established when "the youngster's standardized achievement score fell at least 1.5 standard deviations below the highest obtained intelligence measure." For determining the presence of emotional handicap, "operationalized procedures start with the compilation of specific behavioral data collected over a period of time by the referral source." Also required are direct observation of the youngster by someone other than the referral source, a health screening, and social and educational histories. The test batteries to be used "should include an achievement measure, two behavior checklists, an intelligence measure and two other measures of psychological functioning" (pp. 15-16).

Another example: The Illinois regulations (Illinois Office of Education, 1979) calls for a "Comprehensive Case Study Evaluation." This shall include, but need not be limited to:

1. An interview with the child
2. Consultation with the child's parents
3. A social developmental study, including an assessment of the child's adaptive behavior and cultural background
4. A report regarding the child's medical history and current health status
5. A vision and hearing screening, completed at the time of the evaluation or within the previous six months
6. A review of the child's academic history and current educational functioning
7. An educational evaluation of the child's learning pro-

cesses and level of educational achievement
8. An assessment of the child's learning environment
9. Specialized evaluations specific to the nature of the child's problems.
  9.1. A psychological evaluation by a certified school psychologist, with the extent to be determined by the individual situation, shall be required:
    9.1.1. In order to place any child in a special education placement for children with mental impairment ....
    9.1.2. In order to place any child in a special education instructional program
    9.1.3. In order to place any child in a special education placement for children with behavior disorders
    9.1.4. In order to place any child where there are questions about his or her intellectual functioning and/or learning capacity (pp. 8–10)

For the most part, the state plans called for a fact gathering about the physical and mental condition and the educational functioning of handicapped children that was much more complete and inclusive than any that had been assembled before. It gave the promise of providing much better educational opportunities than had ever been available in most states. A great deal of effort was made, in the years immediately following the enactment of P.L. 94-142, to acquaint teachers and parents with the IEP, its intent, and its processes, for these required attention to the needs of handicapped children that had not been considered before. It must be remembered that the federal law required not only the evaluation of the child's educational condition but the setting of short-term objectives and annual goals and reports on specific educational services and the extent to which these met the requirements of "least restrictive environment." In addition, parents or their surrogates were to be included in the planning for the child and were entitled to the results of the annual reviews and evaluations.

The burdens upon teachers, particularly the special education teachers, were recognized but generally discounted. It is almost amusing to read the memorandum issued by one state's education department in an attempt to meet these problems (Taylor, 1978, pp. 9, 14). It began: "Dear Teachers: Before your arms are extended in despair over the planning and writing of individualized educational programs, certain assumptions should be clarified." Several pages later the memorandum continued:

> The purpose of the IEP is not to cause teachers to "wade through paper". . . . The individual plan . . . offers nothing new, no magical formulas, no novel recipes, no bag of tricks, not even new terminology. It does, however, offer something competent teachers have always used—"common sense" programming . . . Your task, then, will be to translate information into performance objectives and program experiences which will increase the opportunity of meeting needs of children. You will then document your planning, your continual assessment of needs, the hard work of shaping behavior, and the model of self that you portray in moving exceptional children from levels of dependence to levels of independence.

In another state, the regulations include: "Prior to placement, individually sequenced instructional objectives must be developed for each pupil and kept on file by the special teacher receiving the child. Lastly, we are suggesting written concurrence by a state or community mental health center for placement of an EH [emotionally disturbed] child" (Evans, 1979, p. 16).

One of the major requirements of P.L. 94-142 is that parents must be given the opportunity of participating in the educational planning for handicapped children, especially in the preparation of the IEP. In various wordings in their regulations, the states make provision for such participation. Where the parent is not available to attend the meeting of the special education committee at which his or her child is to be discussed, arrangements are made for representation for the child (sometimes by a social worker, sometimes by a designated "child advocate" member of the committee). Across the spectrum of all handicapping conditions there seems to have been good participation by parents in the meetings on IEPs.

PLACEMENT

The Special Education Committee, or Committee on the Handicapped, has the responsibility of designating the kind of special education program to which the child will be assigned. Public Law 94-142 Sect. 1412 defines this as "specially designed instruction, at no cost to parents or guardians, to meet the unique needs of a handicapped child, including classroom instruction, instruction in physical education, home instruction, and instruction in hospitals and institutions." The states have tailored this wording to fit their own structure and resources. New York, for example, defines special education as "specifically designated instruction at no cost to the parent to meet the unique needs of a handicapped child, including special class instruction, resource program instruction, instruction in physical education and home instruction" (New York State Education Law, 1979, Chapter 853).

In New York State the special education programs available are listed as follows:

Special classes

Part-time programs

Resource rooms

Alternate learning centers

Home instruction and special teachers

Contracts with special services or programs

Contracts with private nonresidential schools within or outside the state

Contracts with private residential schools within or outside the state

Assignment to a state or state-supported school

Massachusetts lists its special education programs as follows:

Regular educational program with necessary modifications

Regular educational program with 25% of the individual's time spent receiving special services in another room

Regular educational program with 25 to 60% of the handicapped individual's time spent receiving special services in another room

Substantially separate program

Day school program

Residential school program

Home or hospital

Parent-child

Diagnostic

The Massachusetts regulations state that "a *substantially separate program* functions as a remedial or transition class; the purpose being to prepare the individual to enter or return to a regular education program" (Rittenhouse, 1980, pp. 7-8). It should be kept in mind that according to the federal law and regulations a guiding principle in placement of handicapped children is that they be in the "least restrictive environment." This requirement has had a great effect in forcing the Committees on the Handicapped to consider first the option of placing a handicapped youngster in a regular classroom with or without modifications, a method usually referred to as "mainstreaming." Before I discuss further this and other options, I should like to present two other educational program types that have had a pronounced effect upon services to handicapped persons—vocational education and career education.

VOCATIONAL EDUCATION

Many handicapped youngsters of high school age who have failed in or who have difficulty in dealing with the standard academic curriculum have been helped to move into, or been shunted into, a vocational education program. To some educators vocational education appears to be less intellectually demanding, though vocational educators would challenge this, and to some the preparation for a trade has special value for persons who have trouble in following the usual pattern of schooling. For many mentally ill or emotionally disturbed youngsters who are difficult to manage in regular academic classrooms, vocational courses are often recommended as an alternative.

Vocational education has a long history in the United States. The Smith-Hughes Act of 1917 (P.L. 64-347) provided for the introduction of vocational trade courses in the public school systems. However, it was not until Congress passed the Vocational Education Act of 1963 (P.L. 88-210) that a permanent authority was established and provision was made for funding to construct area vocational schools, work-study programs, and demonstration projects. Amendments in 1968 (P.L. 90-576) required each state to earmark 10% of its vocational education allotment to serve handicapped students who "because of their disabling condition, were unable to succeed in regular vocational educational classes without special educational assistance" (U.S. Department of Education, 1980, p. 22). Education amendments in 1976 (P.L. 94-482) brought the vocational education for handicapped children in line with the provisions of P.L. 94-142, requiring that 50% of the set-aside funds for vocational education come from the states, and that emphasis be placed upon reducing the number of handicapped students in segregated vocational classes. In 1990 Congress passed the Carl D. Perkins Vocational/Applied Technology Education Act. This legislation increases the control of local educational agencies, area schools, and community colleges over vocational educational funding; provides for better cooperation and coordination between high schools and community colleges; and makes for better targeting on special populations, including the economically disadvantaged and the handicapped. It also changes the name from vocational education to "vocational and applied technology" (NARF, 1990b).

The occupational education field extols the value of vocational-technical education as meeting the needs of disadvantaged and handicapped persons. According to the New York State Education Department (1990), about 3 million secondary and postsecondary disadvantaged and handicapped students in the United States are served in these programs each year. In New York State, about one third of the vocational education students are disadvantaged and approximately 10% are designated as handicapped. Though there has always been a tendency for educators, and parents, to look upon vocational education as something less than quality education, the programs have been highly popular with legislators. The Carl D. Perkins Vocational/Applied Technology Education Act (P.L. 98-524) has recently been reauthorized by Congress until 1998.

In educational parlance, handicapped students are considered, along with disadvantaged students, minority students, and students for whom English is a second language, as "students at risk." The risk referred to particularly is that of dropping out of school before completing elementary or secondary education. It is the contention of the vocational educators that occupational education (a term used interchangeably with vocational education) "can serve as a motivator for keeping students in school. A study conducted by the New York City Board of Education found that students who were enrolled in programs at the vocational high schools had a far greater chance of remaining in school than students who

applied to the vocational high school and were not accepted."
In fact, an audit report of the State Controller's Office showed
that New York City's vocational high schools have a lower
pupil dropout rate than its academic high schools (New York
State Education Department, 1987b, 1989, p. 17).

Vocational educational studies also support the claim that
students who graduate from occupational education are much
more likely to be employed. "Less than a half-percent of the
vocational graduates who don't seek postsecondary education
remain jobless, while nearly 17 percent of the dropouts suffer
chronic unemployment" (New York State Education Department, 1989, p. 4). Dunham (1986) refers to an exploratory
study that showed that 29% of handicapped youth who had
vocational training in high school were unemployed compared to 46% of those without such training. Most pertinent to
the question of academic learning by emotionally disturbed
youngsters, which I shall discuss later, is Dunham's finding
that "there is only a very *slight tendency* for students who take
many vocational courses *to take fewer courses in academic
subjects* such as math, English, science, social studies, and
foreign languages" (p. 2).

One of the requirements of the Carl D. Perkins Vocational
Education Act (P.L. 98-524) is that school districts receiving
funds under this act must conduct vocational assessments for
students with handicapping conditions who are enrolled in
occupational education programs. "This assessment must be
sufficient to identify vocational interests, abilities, and special
needs, with consideration given to each student's specific
handicapping condition, to assure successful completion of
the occupational education program. School districts must
also provide information concerning occupational education
opportunities to students with handicapping conditions and

their parents no later than the ninth grade" (BOCES, 1989, p. 1).

This requirement fits naturally into the evaluation provisions of the Individualized Education Program. Many states include special reference to vocational education in their instructions to the Committees on Special Education (CSEs). For example, New York requires:

> that the school district carefully consider the inclusion of occupational education courses and activities in the IEP based on individual student characteristics. The IEP should include prevocational or vocational components, as appropriate, throughout the student's school experience; but consideration of such program options becomes especially important beginning in the early secondary grades. Prior to recommending occupational education programs, the CSE must consider the appropriateness of conducting a vocational assessment. The CSE decision to recommend specific occupational education sequences should be based on the results of the vocational assessment and the individual strengths, needs and interests of the student. (BOCES, 1989, p.1)

It would be nice to say that in developing the IEP, particularly for older adolescents, careful consideration is usually given to the vocational assessment. The truth is that such an occupational evaluation is rarely part of the IEP. In an effort to deal with this lack, a technical advisory committee for the New York State Council on Vocational Education (1989) recommended,

> Provide the CSE with accurate data based upon appropriate

assessments to be used in developing the student's Phase I Individualized Education Program (IEP). CSE process should be modified as follows:

1. Add an occupational education representative as a committee member.
2. The student's prospective occupational education instructor should provide input (individual objectives) prior to placement in occupational education and completion of the Phase I Individualized Education Program (IEP).
3. The occupational education teacher should provide information to be considered by the CSE at the time of annual review.

Make certain a *mentor* is assigned to be responsible for the student on an individual basis and to coordinate the student's total program including occupational education. (pp. 9.1-9.2)

There are manuals of procedure for the preparation of a vocational assessment. In general, these follow the same format as is used in a vocational evaluation in the field of rehabilitation of persons with disabilities. (For a concise description of the process see Black 1988.) In general, in addition to an interest inventory; measures of performance in perception, motor ability, spatial discrimination, and comprehension; and tests of intelligence and verbal and numerical performance, use is often made of commercially developed vocational evaluation instruments. All of the better vocational schools and programs I have visited use the vocational assessment to chart progress of their students and to plan for job seeking and job placement. However, as the BOCES (1989) manual says: "The major obstacle to completing a successful vocational assessment is rarely the instrument or approach used, but most often the lack of training, preparation, and support for the individual responsible for conducting the vocational evaluation" (p. 2).

Vocational education is, of course, intended to provide the youngster with skills directly usable in the work world. For this reason, such training often does have an allure for children who find the going rough in the academic classroom. Many adolescents with limited attention span and lack of interest in reading and arithmetic in regular school do learn these very subjects when the material is linked to what they consider relevant to learning job skills. Unfortunately, I have seen too many vocational courses being taught by instructors who have never been, or were too long ago, exposed to the current methodology or procedures of the workaday world; and there are too many instances in which instruction is given on equipment and with tools already antiquated by developments in the business or industry in which the students will be expected to find jobs.

Nevertheless, increasing linkages with industry and business and with the vocational rehabilitation field show promise of bettering these deficits. These will be discussed in a later chapter.

CAREER EDUCATION

The Council for Exceptional Children (1979) recommended that "career education should be integrated into each handicapped child's individualized education program. In addition to career education experiences, handicapped youngsters should be assisted by guidance and counseling personnel" (p. 4). The U.S. Commissioner of Education, Dr. Sidney Marland, had introduced the concept of career education as federal policy in 1971. Congress then acted to pass P. L. 93-380, which set up an Office of Career Education and a National Advisory Council on Career Education. According to Corthell and Van Boskirk (1984, p. 16) Dr. Kenneth Hoyt, appointed in charge of the new Office of Career Education, defined education as the totality of experiences through which one learns. "Therefore," said Hoyt, "a generic definition of *career education* is the totality of experiences through which one learns about and prepares to engage in work as part of his or her way of living" (Hoyt 1975; Hoyt et al., 1976, p. 16). The intent was to make career education very broad and integrated into the curricula of existing courses from early education on. In the older grades the idea was to provide career education by having the student spend a few hours each week at a work site. As a member of the New York State Advisory Council on Career Education, I recall much discussion and many examples of incorporating material about the work world into courses in English, math, social studies, and even the humanities, but by 1980 the interest seemed to have run its course. There is today little mention of special career materials for education of the handicapped, except in relation to vocational education.

LEAST RESTRICTIVE ENVIRONMENT— MAINSTREAMING

The greatest change that P.L. 94-142 (Education for All Handicapped Children Act) made in educational methodology was in the requirement that children be educated in "the least restrictive environment." This was recognition that many, if not most, of the children considered handicapped could, with adequate support and guidance, remain in regular classrooms and partake of the same teaching as children without handicaps. It should be remembered that this education law was passed in the 1970s, when public attitudes and social philosophy were changing, particularly with regard to the mentally retarded and the physically disabled. These were the days of "normalization" and of "deinstitutionalization" of the mentally impaired and the mentally ill. The changing emphasis in public education was on "mainstreaming."

In an analysis of variations in special education among the states, Danielson and Bellamy (1987) point out that "the least restrictive environment provision of Public Law 94-142 creates a presumption in favor of educating children with handicaps in regular education environments . . . in the setting that is least removed from the regular education environment and that offers the greatest interaction with children who are not handicapped" (p. 1). However, as Shore (1986) explains in his excellent guide for parents, "It has often been misread as a mandate for the transfer of special education students to regular education (or 'mainstream') settings regardless of their needs. Congress never intended such an interpretation" (p. 7).

In 1979 the ERIC Clearinghouse on Handicapped and Gifted Children issued a fact sheet on the responsibilities of regular classroom teachers for handicapped students (Barreal & Mack, 1979). In it they list the following as "some of the things regular educators may be responsible for or be involved in":

Identifying potentially handicapped children.

Referring potentially handicapped children.

Taking part in due process procedures.

Collecting data about handicapped children.

Assisting handicapped children with special equipment.

Participating at IEP meetings.

Participating in team work with other professionals.

Communicating with parents.

Helping handicapped and nonhandicapped children work and play together. (p. 38)

Notwithstanding this list, the fact sheet states, "Whenever a handicapped child is placed in a regular classroom, the responsibility of the regular educator for that child is the same as for any other child in the classroom." The fact sheet goes on to say:

Special education, which involves significant modifications in methodology, curriculum, or environment, may also be delivered to some handicapped children in regular classrooms. Whenever this arrangement is specified in the child's IEP, the development of such specially designed instruction is the responsibility of special educators. Regular educators are responsible for assisting the child in carrying out the program. Overall classroom management also continues to be the responsibility of the regular educator. (p. 38)

It is insisted on the fact sheet that regular classroom teachers already possess some of the skills necessary to work with handicapped children but may need additional:

> Knowledge and use of supplementary aids and services such as brailled worksheets for blind students or provision of tape recorders or typewriters for children who cannot write.
>
> Ability to make minor modifications in schedules.
>
> Use of cooperative teaching techniques in conjunction with special educators.
>
> Knowledge of federal, state, and local policies and procedural requirements.
>
> Operation of physical aids used by the children such as wheelchairs, walkers, and hearing aids. (p. 89)

The regulations of P.L. 94-142 make it clear that only a special educator, with "state educational agency approved or recognized certification, licensing, registration or other comparable requirements which apply to the area in which he or she is providing special education or related services" is qualified to provide special education. The regulations do require the states to develop inservice training for regular teachers in three areas. These are the management of disability in the classroom, understanding of disabilities and their own feelings and biases concerning people who are handicapped, and their relationship to special education. It is understandable that many classroom teachers, responsible for 20 to 35 children, are less than enthusiastic about taking on these additional responsibilities for one or two, or even up to six, special education students.

While there is strong endorsement on all sides of the concept of mainstreaming, there are still, after more than 15 years of P.L. 94-142, great gaps in its implementation. The study by Danielson and Bellamy (1987) revealed that "the average state places nearly five times as many students in segregated settings as do these five states [the five that place the fewest students in segregated settings]" (p. 6). The International Center for the Disabled survey (ICD, 1989) found that "emotionally disturbed (31%), mentally retarded (12%), and multi-handicapped students (9%) are the least integrated into regular classrooms," and that "learning disabled (70%), speech impaired (59%), and visually handicapped children (59%) are the most integrated into regular classrooms" (p. 8). A special review of the New York City school system's use of mainstreaming for handicapped children (Chancellor, 1987) reported that its results were "disheartening and, indeed, disturbing. One area of particular concern is the very small number of youngsters for whom mainstreaming is recommended and, subsequently, those within that group who actually receive the service" (p. 1). The ICD survey (1989) reported that classroom teachers countrywide, on the average, have three or four handicapped children in their classes for all or part of each day, yet only 40% of these teachers have had any training in special education, and only 32% "are very confident about the handicapped students" (p. 8). While 53% of the special education teachers reported that mainstreaming or integration had been "very helpful" for handicapped students, only 36% of the regular classroom teachers thought so.

RESOURCE ROOMS AND SPECIAL CLASSES

At best, the seriously emotionally disturbed youngsters, who are among the least integrated into regular academic classes, are assigned to "resource rooms" in the public schools for all or part of each day. Here they may receive tutoring in academic subjects or help in developing learning and study skills. In illustration, according to the regulations of the New York City Board of Education, "Students who do not demonstrate significant academic difficulties but have significant emotional and social difficulties which prevent appropriate learning performance" may be placed in a "self-contained class in a high school" (New York City Board of Education, 1984, p. 92). What is called the "Basic 2 programming" is "designed to teach independent living such as time, money, measurement, survival reading, travel training, etc. In Basic 2 students receive a functional life skills course of study in the areas of reading, writing, math, social studies, science, and career skills" (p. 90). For less emotionally disturbed students, and among these may be included many children labeled learning disabled, there is a "Basic 1 program" designed for those headed for a high school diploma or certificate. The content of Basic 1 "may reflect a combination of mainstream classes, modified/parallel classes or remedial classes" (p. 90). These special classes are supposedly designed to allow students, when ready, to move into the less restrictive mainstream program with resource room availability. However, as a report to the mayor of New York City asserted, "once labeled 'handicapped,' virtually all students stay in special education the remainder of their school careers, often isolated from their peers and subject to lowered expectations of achievement, fewer educational opportunities and depressed self-images" (New York City, 1987, p. 1).

More restrictive, even, than these special classes are special centers or special schools. In the New York City program these school settings are for:

those seriously emotionally disturbed students who have
demonstrated an inability to function in a less restrictive
environment. . . . For *adolescent students* . . . the student
must demonstrate severe academic difficulties (even with
curricula adaptations and modifications) which prevent the
student from meeting the requirements for a high school
diploma. . . . These academic difficulties cannot be primarily attributable to cultural, linguistic, or ethnic factors; and
cannot be only attributable to erratic school attendance,
prolonged absence from instruction, or recent arrival to
formal public schooling. These educational needs require
specialized instruction on a full-time basis in a self-contained setting. (pp. 175-178)

Class sizes are set at 10 students, with one teacher and a
teacher's aide. There is provision in the regulations for movement of the students to less restrictive programs as they
improve academically and in behavior (New York City Board
of Education, 1984, pp. 89-94, 161-180). This rarely hap-
pened, however; the special report to the mayor pointed out
that in the 1983-84 school year only 2% of all special education students actually reentered regular education (New York
City, 1987).

I would agree with Shore's (1986) contention that "since
secondary school may be a youngster's last experience with
formal education, secondary special educators need to adopt
a broader focus than just imparting basic academic skills. The
needs of their students may require that they also provide
instruction in vocational, daily-living, and social skills" (p.
125). In its report to Congress in 1986, the U.S. Department of
Education said, "The population of SED (severely emotionally disturbed) students presents an extremely complex array
of human service needs. These needs often go beyond the need
for special education, and may include counseling, therapy,

residential requirements, and social service needs. Unless services for this population are coordinated across agencies and with professionals, the effectiveness of each component is jeopardized" (p. 1). In their review of the services to emotionally disturbed youngsters under P.L. 94-142, Friedman and Duchnowski (1987) add: "While day treatment programs that combine mental health, special education, and family services have been demonstrated to be effective in keeping many youngsters out of residential care, such services are often lacking. As a result, children may enter more restrictive placements than they actually need" (p. 2). It may just be that so far as the mentally ill/emotionally disturbed youngsters are concerned, it is too much to expect local educational systems to meet these needs alone without help from other social institutions. What can be done will be the subject of a later chapter.

THE ROLE OF PARENTS

One of the most significant provisions of the Education for All Handicapped Children Act (P.L. 94-142) is the role of parents, guardians, and parent surrogates in the special education process. The regulations require parent participation in arriving at the Individualized Education Program and for written parental consent to the placement decisions reached. In fact, before a school district even proposes to change the placement of a child, the parent must be notified (see Shore, 1986, p. 77). As the Illinois regulations state, for example, "Parents or guardians of an exceptional child must be notified in writing when the local school district proposes *or refuses* to initiate or change the identification, evaluation or educational placement of the child or provision of a free appropriate public education to the child" (Illinois Office of Education, 1979, p. 10). Parents must be notified of the IEP meeting affecting their child. If a parent cannot be present, provision is usually made for a surrogate or parent advocate to attend on behalf of the child. The Illinois provisions are: "If neither parent can attend, the local district shall use other methods to insure parent participation, including individual or conference telephone calls." The local school district must have a detailed written record of its attempts to arrange a mutually acceptable time and place of meeting.

The federal regulations (National Association of State Boards of Education, 1979, p. 20) require that:

> each state must establish procedures to assure that handicapped children and their parents are guaranteed procedural safeguards. These must assure that:
>
> 1. Parents have the right to examine records;
> 2. Parents have the opportunity to obtain an independent evaluation;
> 3. Parents have the right to appeal to a due process hearing officer any decision made by a public education agency.

Furthermore, "a parent has the right to an independent educational evaluation at public expense if the parent disagrees with an evaluation obtained by the LEA (Local Educational Authority)." If, after a hearing, the evaluation is adjudged to be appropriate, the parent "still has the right to an independent educational evaluation, but not at public expense, and the results of this independent evaluation must be considered by the LEA in the decision-making process concerning the child."

A nationwide survey by Louis Harris and Associates (ICD, 1989) revealed that 79% of the parents directly involved attended IEP conferences and an additional 2% were represented by social workers or another parent. Nevertheless, the almost 20% of the parents who did not participate is a high minority, and one must wonder whether parents of emotionally disturbed children are more highly represented in this part of the total, particularly as these parents in the same survey reported the lowest rate of satisfaction with the special education systems for their children.

The Harris survey (ICD, 1989) also showed that while 77% of the parents of handicapped children reported they were satisfied with the special education system, "only a small proportion of parents of handicapped children are knowledgeable about their rights" (p. 5).

CIVIL RIGHTS

A number of federal laws assure protection of children, and particularly handicapped children, in public educational programs from discrimination because of race, color, national or ethnic origin, or handicapping condition. Most far reaching in importance in this regard has been the Civil Rights Act of 1964, Title VI, Section 601. In 1972 the Office of Civil Rights issued a memorandum to chief state and local school district officers and superintendents on "The Elimination of Discrimination in the Assignment of Children to Special Education Classes for the Mentally Retarded." This memorandum stated, "A school district which assigns students to special education classes for the mentally retarded must be prepared to insure that cultural factors unique to the particular race or national origin of the student being evaluated, which may effect the results of test findings with regard to adaptive behavior, are adequately accounted" (Evans, 1979, p. 5). It was followed by provisions of Title IX of the Education Amendments of 1972 (P.L. 92-318), which prohibited discrimination on the basis of sex in educational programs and in activities benefiting from federal financial assistance. In 1973, Title V of the Rehabilitation Act included as Section 504 the prohibition of discrimination against qualified disabled persons in all institutions receiving federal financial assistance. The definition of handicapped in this legislation is more general than in P.L. 94-142, and adds such impairments as alcoholism and drug addiction. Section 504, as civil rights legislation, has no expiration date.

Local educational authorities have the responsibility of compliance with Section 504 as well as with the antidiscrimination provisions of P.L. 94-142, monitored by their state educational agencies. Parents and others have access to "due process" procedures in the various states, including hearings and recourse to the courts if claims of discrimination are made. (See National Association of State Boards of Education, 1979, pp. 20-21; Shore, 1986.)

The latest addition to civil rights legislation for people who have handicaps is the Americans with Disabilities Act of 1990 (P.L. 101-336). For the handicapped youngsters with whom we are here concerned, the most important sections of the act are Title I, dealing with employment, and Title III: Public Accommodations and Services Operated by Private Entities. Title I states, "No covered entity shall discriminate against a qualified individual with a disability because of the disability of such individual in regard to job application procedures, the hiring, advancement, or discharge of employees, employee compensation, job training, and other terms, conditions, and privileges of employment" (P.L. 101-336). Title III prohibits discrimination in public accommodations, whether publicly or privately operated; the intent is "to bring individuals with disabilities into the economic and social mainstream of American life." The advantages to youngsters moving from school into the work world should be obvious.

REPORT CARD ON THE SYSTEM

After more than a decade of experience with P.L. 94-142 and with state laws and regulations purporting to provide education for all handicapped children, strong opinions have evolved as to the success of the enterprise. Weintraub (1987), writing in the *Newsletter* of the American Psychological Association, says:

> P.L. 94-142 and the special education system which it governs have been perhaps the most studied human services delivery system that exists. These myriad of studies demonstrate a number of positive accomplishments that can be summarized in the following fashion:
>
> > handicapped children are being identified earlier;
> >
> > children who were previously unserved are being served and those who were underserved are being educated more appropriately; and
> >
> > special education programming is more comprehensive in terms of the options available to children and youth, both in terms of placement and professional services. (p. 1)

Professor Alan Gartner, of the Graduate School of the City University of New York, in a telephone interview with the *New York Times* (1988), "acknowledged that the law had been 'massively successful' in important respects. Since the law took effect, the number of handicapped students in public schools has increased by more than 650,000, to 4.4 million, or about 11 percent of the total enrollment. In addition, Federal spending on special education has increased sharply, to $1.6 billion in the fiscal year 1985 from $100 million in the fiscal year 1976" (p. B5).

The Harris poll previously referred to (ICD, 1989, p. 6) reported that "educators believe that the education of children with handicapping conditions has improved" and that "the majority of parents of handicapped children (77%) also report that they are satisfied with the special education system." The survey also found that "most parents give their children's schools positive ratings on key criteria (e.g., the attitude of educators toward parents of handicapped children, physical access to school facilities, and efforts to integrate handicapped and non-handicapped children in school activities). . . . Educators agree with parents . . . although they generally tend to be more positive than parents."

On the other hand, there are a number of specific criticisms. In the Harris survey (ICD, 1989), "A substantial number of educators, e.g., 38% of regular classroom teachers and 30% of district directors of special education, report that there are handicapped students who are either not identified as handicapped or who are not receiving services." At the same time, Professor Gartner (*New York Times*, 1988), and a colleague, Professor Dorothy Kerzner Lipsky complain "that a lack of skills and resources, and prejudice among school professionals, have left large numbers of problem students and minority children who are wrongly labeled 'learning disabled'" (p. B5).

Gartner and Lipsky believe that "the way students were evaluated as learning disabled and placed in special education classes was largely arbitrary." They say that:

> the number of students categorized by school systems as learning-disabled rose 119 percent from the 1975-76 school year to the 1984-85 school year, although the total number of students enrolled in special education classes increased by only 16 percent. They attribute the increase in part to the pressure on public schools to have students do well on systemwide and national tests, and in part to the contention of special education professionals that they are best able to educate disabled students. (p. B5)

These opinions, by the way, are shared by mental health professionals with whom I have discussed the matter, and, as I have indicated earlier, I, too, believe that many behaviorally disordered youngsters are labeled learning disabled.

Other criticisms pertain to the programming decisions by the Special Education Committees, the involvement of parents in this process, the preparation of transition to the workaday world, the availablity of related services, and the training of teachers. Friedman and Duchnowski (1987), writing about services for severely emotionally disturbed children, state:

> Despite the requirements of P.L. 94-142 that an individualized educational plan be developed for all students, there is little indication that educational programming and curricula have really been individualized to meet these needs.... While there have been increases in the number of federally

funded training and information projects directed towards
parents of handicapped children, there is still inadequate
involvement of parents in planning for the needs of their
SED children. (p.3)

The report to the mayor of New York City (1987, p. viii) said,
"With few exceptions, students in New York City's public
schools are placed in programs based on the availability of a
program and not according to individual skills and interests."
I am sure that program availability does condition placement
options in many, if not most, school districts. It is not logical
to expect that new or expensive placement arrangements will
be devised to meet the needs of a few special students.

Severe criticisms are presented with regard to the provisions for preparing handicapped students for the work world.
The Harris survey (ICD, 1989, p. 6) found that in evaluating
the school system both parents and teachers gave lowest
ratings to:

preparing handicapped students for work or further study
beyond high school. . . . Only 11% of parents and 15% of
educators say that the schools do an excellent job in
preparing students for jobs after high school. Only 15% of
parents and educators say that schools do an excellent job
in preparing students for education beyond high school....
For a majority of handicapped students aged 17 or over,
transition plans designed to assist them in moving from
school to work have not been made part of the IEP. In
addition, only 33% of the parents with children aged 17 or
over who have post-secondary transition plans say these
plans were carried out. Less than half of the students aged
17 and over have received counseling concerning employment or further educational plans. . . . Substantial numbers

of both educators and parents feel that the schools could be more effective in assisting handicapped students during times of transition.

Even in a large school system with a variety of options, such as that of New York City, the report is that "the Division of High Schools must do a better job of placing students in programs which fit their aptitudes and interests, particularly in the vocational area. . . . Programs rarely link students to job opportunities, and there are few job counselors to help special education students find employment after leaving school" (New York City, 1987, p. viii). A study of learning-disabled and behavior-disordered graduates of greater Chicago high schools (Messerer & Meyers, 1983) revealed that the learning-disabled graduates particularly reported that there was a need for more specific job training in their school sojourn. The researchers felt that "curriculum that focuses exclusively on the 'remediation' of academic deficiencies most likely fails to prepare the LD for what he will need to be able to do in order to survive in the adult world" (p. 11).

On a more positive note, Fairweather (1989), in a country-wide sample of 1,549 secondary school districts stratified by enrollment, geographic region, and district/community wealth, found that:

more than 50% of all secondary LEAs provide at least one of four vocational preparation programs for handicapped students. . . . Large and small LEAs are about equally likely to have a VR (vocational rehabilitation) staff member assigned to them or to provide counseling services for special education students. . . . About one-third of the LEAs

> say they have a staff member whose main function is to
> assist handicapped students find jobs. About 45% claim
> they have a transition program . . . larger LEAs are more
> likely than smaller ones to provide services. (p. 316)

Nevertheless, Bellamy and Wilcox (1981) had found that
many secondary LEAs focus only on the academic performance of special education students and not on preparation for
the world of work.

As I mentioned in relation to mainstreaming, an important
criticism is the lack of adequate training of regular teachers to
deal with children with handicaps. As the Harris survey (ICD,
1989, p. 5) pointed out, "Thirteen years after the passage of
P.L. 94-142, the majority of both principals and teachers have
not had adequate training in special education, and many are
not very confident in making decisions concerning handicapped children." Among the recommendations of Gartner
and Lipsky (*New York Times*, 1988) is "that all teachers be
more broadly trained so that more of them can effectively
teach all kinds of students in the same classroom" (p. B5).

SUMMATION

In summation, it is important to recognize just how much has
actually been accomplished in the decade and a half that the
Education for All Handicapped Children Act has been in
effect. Thousands of children with disabilities have benefited
from the resources provided and educational options and
opportunities developed, where none existed before. Both
regular classroom and special education teachers and school
supervisory and management personnel have devoted more
energy to and exhibited more concern for handicapped children than they ever did before. There has been a heightened

consciousness about handicap and disability and a greater willingness by nonhandicapped people to recognize the strengths and abilities of the disabled, rather than, as in the past, to concentrate on their limitations as though they had no abilities at all.

Many changes in educational processes have been required (including the IEP, evaluations, legal parental involvement in education, special placement procedures, special classroom methods). If we think of the tortoiselike pace at which social change usually takes place, it would seem that education of the handicapped has emulated the hare instead!

The major benefit of these changes in education, I believe, has been mostly to those traditionally recognized as disabled—the physically handicapped, the blind, the deaf, and to a lesser extent the mildly and moderately mentally retarded. The disabled youngsters I am discussing here are really new to educational policy—except in its prior exclusion of them. I believe that it will take more time for public education to catch up with their needs. This is because it is still difficult for the educational community, and the ordinary citizen, to wholly accept that children whose behavior is disorderly really *deserve* an education, and also because it may actually not be possible for educational agencies alone to supply the resources to make education available and accessible to youngsters who are emotionally disturbed/mentally ill. The next two chapters will highlight the roles of the treatment world and the world of work and employment in helping to meet the educational needs of these handicapped adolescents and young adults.

CHAPTER 4

TEACHING AND TREATMENT

While children and adolescents labeled as mentally ill, emotionally disturbed, or behaviorally disordered are educationally the responsibility of special education, they ipso facto have been classified (diagnosed) as ill and therefore also require medical (or psychological) attention. Except with children with the most extremely disordered behaviors, the tendency on the part of school authorities, as well as parents, is to leave it to the schools to deal with the youngster's daily problems. What a *New York Times* (1991) article said recently about the education of poor children applies equally to those who are handicapped:

> What America expects of its public schools these days is nothing less than miracles. Never mind that the children who show up for their first day of kindergarten may have lived their five years in chaos. Give them a good teacher, a

decent classroom and an introduction to the alphabet, the reasoning goes, and those children should be on their way out of poverty and into productivity. Not true. It will take a lot more than a strengthened school system, desirable though that may be.

SCHOOL APPROACHES

School systems have developed a number of approaches to deal with emotionally disturbed youngsters. I have mentioned the increased use of mainstreaming for those who can be contained within a regular classroom. Most usually this is with the aid of a resource room to which the handicapped student can be sent for special tutoring in academic subjects or for instruction in "activities of daily living." Sometimes provision is made for the use of a "consultant teacher." The consultant teacher may attend the pupil with a handicapping condition in the regular classroom to "aid such pupil to benefit from the regular education program" (Newsbrief, 1988-89). At times, the consultation is provided to the regular education teachers to help them in changing the learning environment or modifying their instructional methods to meet the needs of the pupils with handicaps who are in their classes. It is intended that such consultation be given by trained special education teachers, and this is so specified in the educational regulations of some states. In practice, however, often the consultant teacher who visits the classrooms is a paraprofessional with no qualifications in special education. Although such "consultation" will certainly be of help to a regular teacher, for whom the disturbed youngster may be an additional burden, it is questionable as to how much educational assistance is available for the student.

The most usual teaching arrangement for children and adolescents with behavior disorders is a self-contained classroom, whether in a regular school or in a school or center that is removed from the regular public school. In the words of the New York City Board of Education (1984, pp. 93-94), manual for students with handicapping conditions, "Management needs: Based upon the combined academic and social needs, the student requires a smaller instructional group for learning than that provided in general education and constant adult-directed supervision in order to engage in learning. In order to fully participate in the classroom setting, the student requires an additional adult besides the teacher." The hallmark of the special class is its smaller size, 12 pupils in the class in regular school, 10 in the special center or school, and the addition of one or two adults besides the teacher.

Large school systems with sizable numbers of youngsters who present behavior problems have tried setting up special schools, using special education teachers instead of regular teachers, and with smaller class sizes and additional adults for management and security. In New York City some years ago, for example, a number of so-called 600 schools were organized for troubled adolescents. For the most part, these served more as "holding centers" to keep the youngsters off the streets than as true educational institutions, and the 600 schools have gone the way of many an experimental educational trial.

A more successful approach has been the use of special classes in the vocational schools (BOCES—Boards of Cooperative Educational Services) in New York State, outside of the largest cities. Here, the BOCES are set up to serve a group of cooperating school districts, each district paying for the vocational instruction provided children adjudged eligible. A number of such BOCES offer special services to handicapped youngsters, including the emotionally disturbed, who are interested in the vocational subjects being taught. A Suffolk County BOCES I have visited, for example, has such classroom programs in automotive repair and in the production and sale of gardening products and flowers with particular emphasis on serving behaviorally disturbed youngsters.

Residential institutions for delinquent children, many of whom were also emotionally disturbed, have existed since the beginning of the century. Until the midcentury they were mostly conceived of as "training schools" in which a strict discipline and a "conditioned environment" (Alt, 1955; see also Black, 1971) would suffice to place the youngsters on "the right track." In the 1920s and 1930s, August Eichorn (1934) had applied ideas of manipulating the environment to work with disturbed institutionalized children in Vienna; as these ideas were developed "milieu therapy" was adapted to deal with youngsters in institutions directed by such mental health leaders as Fritz Redl at Bellefaire, in Cleveland, and Bruno Bettelheim, at the Orthogenic School in Chicago. Maxwell Jones (1953), in his celebrated work in England during World War II, devised the treatment approach now known as the "therapeutic community," in which the milieu therapy concept was utilized to provide for greater participation by the patients (residents) in controlling their lives in the institution. Therapeutic community meetings have by now become a standard part of the psychiatric treatment methods in many institutions and community mental health centers.

As I indicated in Chapter 1, residential treatment centers either operate their own school systems under the supervision of the state educational authority, or arrange a cooperative program with the public school district in which they are located. An example of the former is the Hawthorne-Cedar Knolls School, mentioned in Chapter 1, the residential treatment unit of the Jewish Board of Family and Children's Services of New York. Another, typical of private residential centers specializing in serving troubled adolescents is the Rocky Mountain Academy in Bonners Ferry, Idaho. Here the emphasis is on providing a complete living, learning, and working environment far removed from the life system from which the youngster comes. The expectation is that students will learn new habit patterns and values that will lead them into more normal and acceptable behavior when they "graduate."

It is important to note that schooling is not the primary responsibility of the residential treatment center, although it is always an important component. As Redick and Witkin (1983) have pointed out, "Residential treatment centers for emotionally disturbed children are a heterogeneous group of mental health facilities which have one characteristic in common, that is, the provision of round-the-clock treatment and care to persons primarily under 18 years of age who are diagnosed as having an emotional or mental disorder" (p. 2). In varying degrees these centers are similar to psychiatric hospitals. In fact, networks of treatment centers with restrictive qualities, from "summer camp" to psychiatric hospital, have been organized under private auspice (e.g., the Devereux and Brown Schools). Since local school districts are unlikely to operate residential treatment facilities, placement of children for whom the Committee on Special Education has recommended more restrictive education has usually been in privately run (nonprofit, profit-making, or charitable) residential schools. Many of these have been outside the local school district, and even outside the state of residence of the child.

Although such residential placement may meet the mental health treatment needs of a youngster at the time, it has its deleterious side. "Placing a youngster in facilities located a considerable distance from his or her community creates problems in maintaining contacts with family, school, and other key persons and agencies in the community. This can be disorienting and disruptive for children, and may also make the transition out of residential treatment, when it does come about, more difficult" (Stroul & Friedman, 1986).

CLASSROOM TECHNIQUES

The manuals of the various state education agencies dealing with special education are replete with instructions for classroom teaching and management of handicapped children. For example, the West Virginia manual recommends (Taylor, 1978, p. 104) that the development of the instructional program should take into account:

1. The significance of the student's individuality and his interactions with the environment.
2. The interrelatedness of the cognitive, affective, physical and psychodynamic developmental areas.
3. Individual planning, implementation and evaluation strategies.
4. Specific programmatic strategies to achieve success based on needs.
5. The establishment of criteria necessary for the development and implementation of that individual's educational program allowing optimal achievement by the child.

This is to be achieved through "effective" teaching and class management, with the following characteristics:

1. *Flexibility*—the ability to use a variety of approaches for meeting specific needs.
2. *Variety*—the ability to present instruction through a variety of methods with a maintenance of interest.
3. *Motivation*—the ability to provide children with a reason to learn with tangible and social reinforcement.
4. *Structure*—the ability to provide needed direction, organization, and teaching.
5. *Success*—the ability to provide opportunity for succeeding.
6. *The Teacher*—the ability to provide needed strategies and results. (pp. 104–105)

The State of Vermont developed the following set of philosophies of education for the handicapped (Taylor, 1978):

1. Education should be based upon the individual's strong inherent desire to learn and make sense of his environment.
2. Educators should strive to maintain the individuality and originality of the learner.
3. Emphasis should be upon a child's own way of learning through the discovery and exploration of real experiences.
4. A child's perception of the learning process should be related to his own concept of reality.
5. A child should be allowed to work according to his own abilities.

6. Expectations of children's progress should be individualized. (p. 113)

As recounted by Taylor, the Indiana School of Education established "The Ten Commandments for Freedom in the Classroom" (Taylor, 1978).

1. Thou shalt be free to choose but remember to accept the consequences.
2. Thou shalt trust and have faith in all children.
3. Thou shalt not use the word FREEDOM in vain, for a child's future will not hold you guiltless.
4. Honor the child that his school days may be so joyous he will cherish the freedom to learn thou hast given him.
5. Thou shalt create an atmosphere of openness and respect.
6. Thou shalt honor each child; remember that he is unique and special and thou shalt facilitate his opportunities to learn in his own way, at his own rate, using his own special interests.
7. Thou shalt make positive efforts to communicate effectively with each student every day.
8. Thou shalt not stifle, suffocate, or inhibit a child's creative or critical thinking process.
9. Thou art as free as thou like until thy freedom restricts someone else's freedom and/or hurts him.
10. Thou shalt respect each child. (p. 112)

One could hardly hope for a more comprehensive, integrative, and child-centered set of philosophies than are included in these state department of education instructions to teachers.

Whether they are translated, or even translatable, into classroom practice for handicapped children, and particularly for emotionally disturbed adolescents, is another matter entirely. Educators who deal with children who are labeled behavior disordered (McIntyre & Brulle, 1989) point out that "the importance of creating an effectively managed classroom environment cannot be overstated. . . . The teacher must successfully orchestrate the events and routines of the day, direct the actions of his or her students, and, when faced with misbehavior, respond in a manner that will allow teaching and learning to continue." How this can be done is suggested by D'Zamko and Hedges (1985; see also Kounin et al., 1966) in categories originally developed in regular classrooms and later replicated with emotionally disturbed pupils. The teacher is asked to develop the following:

1. With-it-ness: the teacher has "eyes in the back of her head"
2. Group alerting: "the teacher tries to sustain pupil attention and keep all pupils involved" (p. 63)
3. Smoothness: the teacher keeps transitions between activities in the classroom flowing in an orderly manner
4. Accountability: "the teacher makes it clear that pupils are to demonstrate involvement in the learning activity"
5. Overlappingness: "the teacher can deal with two or more things at the same time"
6. Seatwork variety: "the teacher's ability to stimulate enthusiasm, involvement, and curiosity by avoiding boredom with more of the same types of activities" (p. 63)

"Behaviorism is the predominant perspective for managing students with behavioral disorders taught in American colleges and universities," reported Bauer and Sapona (1988) in a critique of teaching methods for children with severe behavioral disorders. "From the behavioral perspective," they assert, "students with severe behavioral disorders demonstrate behaviors which can be judged as appropriate or inappropriate, and then increased or decreased through the application of specific technology" (pp. 280-87). For example, as the West Virginia manual (Taylor, 1978) advised under "Special Management Techniques for Teachers": "Grandma's Rule: Many behaviors in which a child will engage can be used to reinforce those behaviors in which he will not readily engage. The teacher must require the less preferred activity before the more preferred activity is allowed (must eat your spinach before dessert)" (p. 234).

An analysis of curriculum practice for learning-disabled secondary school students (Seidenberg, 1986), which in my opinion applies as well to the teaching of the emotionally disturbed, reports:

> The predominant classroom formats used most often by secondary teachers were seat work and lecture followed by some class discussion. There is little student-teacher interaction and minimal feedback is given to students. . . . Students are required to work independently on assignments requiring reading and writing skills. In general, teachers expect that students should have acquired the skills to function independently in a number of areas such as volunteering answers, requesting assistance, locating the correct page(s), and budgeting time without continuous monitoring. (p. 3)

With all the references to broad curriculum content in the manuals for teachers, a recent nationwide study of the best educational programs for children with behavioral and emotional problems (Knitzer et al., 1990) concludes, "The curriculum emphasis is on behavior management first, learning, if at all, second. Central to many of the classrooms that we visited was a great concern with behavioral point systems. Yet often, these seemed largely designed to help maintain silence in the classroom, not to teach children how better to manage their anger, sadness or impulses" (p. xii). In his guide for parents and educators, Shore (1986) says of handicapped high school students, "Since secondary school may be a youngster's last experience with formal education, secondary special educators need to adopt a broader focus than just imparting basic academic skills. The needs of their students may require that they also provide instruction in vocational, daily-living, and social skills" (p. 135). The Bank Street College study (Knitzer et al., 1990) found that "although many of the children identified as behaviorally or emotionally handicapped under the law allegedly 'lack social skills', the school day provides limited and sometimes only artificial opportunities (that is, through specialized curricula that are not integrated into the classroom) for them to master experiences of cooperating with peers, playing sports, participating in extracurricular activities, or even enjoying recess" (p. xiii). Only in very special demonstration programs and in collaborative efforts with rehabilitation agencies, which I shall describe later, is teaching of social skills and activities of daily living (sometimes referred to as "survival skills") regularly integrated with the public school curricula.

TRAINING OF SPECIAL EDUCATORS

All states have requirements for certification or licensure for teachers in special education. In some, a general certificate qualifies a special education teacher to teach children with any handicap; in many, qualifications are restricted to types of handicaps, for example, "speech and hard of hearing," "visual handicaps," "physical disabilities." Frequently qualification for teaching the emotionally disturbed or behaviorally disordered is linked with the right to teach the learning disabled and/or the mildly mentally retarded. Training required is almost always at the master of education level. As Shore (1986) points out, "Because all children act inappropriately on occasion, it takes training and experience to differentiate between those whose behavior falls within the typical range and those whose behavior qualifies as an educational disability which warrants special education" (p. 13).

To answer charges that have been made that there may be a mismatch between preparation for teachers of the severely behavioral disordered and public school practices in educating behaviorally disordered children, Russell and Williams (1984) conducted a study of the competencies required and used. One hundred and sixty-seven educators, including public school administrators and supervisors, regular teachers, special educators, and university teachers of educators, responded to a questionnaire covering 27 competencies determined as important for teachers of the behaviorally disturbed. The results of the study indicated that while all of the 27 competencies were judged to be important for educating severely behaviorally disordered students, 13 of the competencies were insufficiently addressed in teacher training. These

13 included "assessment, interactional programming, facilitating students' social skills, assisting students with medical problems, communication skills for parent/professional interaction, and the ability to mainstream students" (pp. 8–13). Although training in social skills rated sixth in need, it rated 17th in perceived training. As I mentioned earlier, behavior modification is the modality most commonly taught in the educational colleges for managing children with behavior disorders. Russell and Williams (1984, p. 6) refer to surveys showing that the emphasis in teacher training is on behavioral and academic measurement, prescriptive teaching practices, and methods of intervention. Psychodynamic diagnostic and treatment approaches are deemphasized. This may make more difficult the necessary communication between special educators and mental health practitioners. As the Bank Street study (Knitzer et al., 1990) concluded, "In many programs, even those with otherwise strong academic or management components, there is a limited, if any, mental health presence. Children often lack access to therapy and teachers to consultation and support, even in the face of predictable crises" (p. 115).

TREATMENT

Some children who are labeled mentally ill, emotionally disturbed, or behaviorally disordered receive treatment from a psychiatrist, psychologist, or social worker directly or through a mental health clinic or center. The president of the American Psychiatric Association, Dr. Elissa P. Benedeck, estimated that only about 5% of the children in the United States who suffer from mental illness are actually receiving such treatment (Hospital & Community Psychiatry, 1991). It is likely that many more such children, in the public school system, are receiving behavior modification forms of treatment or management from special education teachers in the classroom settings. Most popular has been the use of aversive conditioning or awareness therapy, defined as "a behavior reduction procedure where the stimulus that elicits the maladaptive behavior is repeatedly paired with an aversive stimulus. . . . The purpose of aversion therapy is to make the stimuli that cue the inappropriate behavior unpleasant, thus leading to a reduction in the behavior in question" (Rutherford, 1978, p. 43).

In brief, aversive conditioning is described as including negative reinforcement (e.g., threats), "on-set" punishment (including physical aversives, "overcorrection," verbal aversives such as reprimands), and "off-set" punishment, including "response cost losses" and various forms of "time out." Response cost loss means loss of privileges or loss of promised opportunity to participate in a specified activity, or, in the case of a token economy form of treatment, the removal or loss of tokens. Time out is "a procedure by which access to the sources of reinforcement is removed for a particular time period, contingent upon the omission of a (maladaptive) response" (p. 51). The forms of time out range from ignoring or withholding of adult social attention, through "contingent observation" ("where the child is removed from a reinforcing group or activity for a period of time to a place where he or she can continue to observe the activity but not participate in it"), to removal of materials, reduction of response maintenance stimuli, and, in extreme cases, to exclusion and finally to seclusion (Rutherford, 1978, p. 15).

Rutherford concludes that "the bulk of the current empirical evidence on punishment in the classroom supports the effectiveness of this procedure in suppressing the inappropriate behaviors of children and youth . . . punishment is effective in changing behaviors and that, in fact, punishment plays an important and necessary role in the socialization process" (p. 57). However, in the same volume, Richard Neel (1978) issues a warning with which from my experience I agree, that "punishment works, for a time. The literature strongly supports the effectiveness of punishment in the short run. If, however, a new set of adaptive, competing behaviors are not taught, then the effectiveness of the punishing strategy will diminish or disappear" (p. 79).

In my own experience, many years ago we noted the short-term success of summer camp placement of severely disturbed children and adolescents. A combination of therapeutic community and behavior modification approaches seemed to have the effect of quieting hyperactive children and stimulating withdrawn youngsters. Parents and social workers commented approvingly on the behavior of the children on their return home from camp, but the changes did not last. Interestingly, two recent reports of such experiments confirm this experience. Goldhaber (1991) tells of using a summer day treatment program for children with attention deficit hyperactivity disorder. The results of the 8-week camp placement were very positive. "Improved social skills and reduced oppositional behavior were attributed to the group therapies, behavior management strategies, and parent training. . . . Improvements in self-esteem seemed most related to improved relationships and accomplishments in recreational activities. . . . In their final evaluations, parents made positive comments about the program and, more important, about their children" (p. 424). By the 10-week follow-up, however, some of the children had begun to slip back into earlier behavior.

Jureidini (1991) describes a "living skills" program for adolescents suffering from schizophrenia or affective psychosis that was set up in a psychiatric hospital. The program included creative and crafts work and academic instruction along with such practical living skills as personal care, cooking, and shopping. The average length of stay was about 3 months. Results "indicated that this Living Skills Program was effective in improving mental state and interpersonal functioning in the short term. Yet the outcome at 9 months follow-up was disappointing" (p. 109).

To an increasing extent psychiatric treatment is including the use of pharmacological agents. This is true also in the treatment of children and adolescents, and, as Forness and Kavale (1988) have documented, "School personnel have become increasingly more concerned with the effects of psychotropic medication on school performance" (p. 144). Four major classes of medication are being used: (a) stimulants (e.g., Ritalin), (b) neuroleptics or antipsychotics (major tranquilizers, e.g., Thorazine, mellaril, prolixin, haldol, navane), (c) anticonvulsant medications (e.g., phenobarbital, tegretol, Dilantin, mysoline), and (d) antidepressants (e.g., lithium carbonate, imipramine).

Studies are continuing of the effects of these drugs upon alleviation of symptoms and upon behavior in the classroom. There is some evidence, according to Forness and Kavale (1988), that the use of stimulants, particularly Ritalin, in combination with behavioral interventions is superior to either medication or classroom intervention used alone in quieting hyperactivity, reducing the need for teacher control, and increasing attending behaviors and academic performance.

For children with psychoses, the neuroleptics do gradually reduce agitation or aggression and increase socialization. However, there seems to be a side effect of excessive drowsiness. As these authors conclude:

> Recent educational research on school performance in medication studies has not kept pace with the burgeoning research effort by psychiatrists and pediatricians. These medical researchers are not always aware, nor are their clinical colleagues aware, of the possible problems such pharmacological agents may present in ongoing classroom situations. Teachers and educational researchers, on the other hand, are not always aware of the potentially powerful therapeutic effects of various psychotropic medications on classroom performance. Interdisciplinary collaboration, in both research and clinical practice, seems a particularly critical next step. (p. 147)

The treatment of choice among mental health professionals continues to be psychotherapy. There is a growing interest in the mental health field in adolescence as a stage of life. "Adolescence occupies the attention of professionals as a clinical challenge because of its frequent disruptive aspects, as a developmental period because of its reworking and character synthetic functions, and as a social phenomenon making a large impact on values and social institutions. Experienced professionals believe that the therapeutic tasks with adolescents require special techniques that differentiate adolescent therapy from child and adult treatment" (Feinstein, 1980, p. vii).

Every form of psychodynamic intervention has been used with disturbed adolescents, including individual approaches, group therapies, family therapies, supportive therapies, and behavioral modifications (Esman et al., 1992). As Feinstein (1980) put it, "With our greater understanding of ego development and structural theory ... the development of a wide range of dyadic techniques from supportive dynamic psychotherapy to intensive psychoanalytic psychotherapy and psychoanalysis are now more comfortably utilized" (p. viii). The greatest difficulties are in engaging the troubled youngsters in a therapeutic program in the first place, in marshalling sufficient treatment resources to meet the very great need, and in integrating the treatment processes with these youngsters' educational programs.

CHANGING EDUCATIONAL APPROACHES

Dissatisfaction with our public school educational system seems to be a perennial state in American society. Unhappiness with the results of academic testing, concerns about comparisons with students from other Western economies, horror at the large dropout rates for minority and other socially disadvantaged students, and most lately apprehension about whether we are producing sufficiently educated employees for the next generation have led to a variety of recommendations for changing or at least retooling our educational system. Some of these have been targeted at the system as a whole, affecting all students; some have been concerned primarily with education for handicapped youngsters. Before we turn our attention to the world of work as related to emotionally disturbed or mentally ill young people, it is worth noting some of the changes that have been or are being proposed.

The federal government is on the verge of setting as national policy an experimental approach to standardizing "performance-based achievement" of students (*Science*, 1991). The

National Center on Education and the Economy, in Rochester, New York, and the University of Pittsburgh's Learning Research and Development Center have developed three types of assessments for high schools: "individual 'performance examinations' where students respond to questions from examiners, individual and group projects, and portfolios of student work. Assessments will be tied to a syllabus and set of standards devised by an independent National Education Board" (p. 517). While such a national standard will make it easier to compare achievements across local school board and state lines, it raises questions as to the effect upon "individualized teaching" and teacher autonomy, now being advocated by experts in special education (Daniels, 1988) to meet the needs of handicapped youngsters.

Another general recommendation that has gained popularity is the introduction of experiential education, sometimes referred to as "discovery learning." In essence this focuses teaching around class projects in which the students take on service or fact- gathering roles and in which the role of the teacher changes from that of director and monitor to that of facilitator. Wehlage and associates (1982) in a report to the governor of Wisconsin describe such classes for marginal high school students. They emphasize what they believe is great efficacy in keeping students involved in school. Other proposals with similar structure have been built around "hands-on" or "integrative" teaching for vocational education (The Benchmark, 1989). However, in discussing a similar educational approach utilizing computers as the experiential focus, Henry J. Becker of Johns Hopkins University (*Science*, 1989) advised that most teachers "want technology that will fit into the traditional curriculum. . . . Most are still basically immured in the behaviorist paradigm that guided the earliest attempts at computer aided instruction: the instructor presents the stimulus, the students respond, and are given feedback on whether they are right or wrong. Or . . . teachers treat 'knowledge as fluid' which pour into the student-vessels" (p. 908).

Bauer and Sapona (1988) have proposed for special education teachers of children with behavioral disorders a role similar to that in experiential education. They call it a "facilitative approach" in contrast to the usual teaching role, which they call a "directive" one. They explain, "A facilitative teacher creates learning environments which provide greater opportunities for student participation in communication, in contrast to the highly structured question-answer exchanges found in classrooms. Students initiate and assume the lead in social interactions and participate in a variety of ways" (p. 283). Such a process is intended to lead the students to "more conventional behaviors, that is, behaviors more readily understood and more typically shared by the social community" (p. 283).

The National Center on Education and Employment, of Teachers College, Columbia University, suggests using a team approach in classrooms similar to what has been found successful in Japanese schools. Says Dr. Sue Berryman (1989), "Let's relax another assumption—about how classrooms should be organized. For example, there are many adult situations where team performance—and the individual's ability to perform well within a team—matter *far* more than individual pyrotechnics. However, our schools are organized to develop and grade competence of the individual, not an individual's competence in the group. We *can* change how we organize the work of the classroom" (p. 9).

Another, more general recommendation is that "manual education" become central to the liberal education of all students (Oakes 1986). "A central tenet of this vision is that vocational education would become part of the common curriculum in comprehensive schools. That is, vocational education would be perceived and structured as legitimate 'status knowledge' for all students at all ages (not, as currently, a booby prize for adolescents who can't make it in legitimate knowledge areas)" (p. 65).

Among recommendations specific to the education of behaviorally disordered children are research findings that nonverbal commands by teachers are better understood by the students than verbal ones (McIntyre & Brulle, 1989, pp. 123-131) and also, that by spreading the teaching of daily living skills and vocational preparation over the entire junior high school and high school years an answer could be given to the complaint that "educators had indicated they felt that offering academic as well as vocational instruction taxed the amount of time they had with the students" (Dick, 1985, p. 6).

A newer approach for academically inclined youngsters who are mentally ill or behaviorally disturbed has been developed by the rehabilitation field and called "supported education" (Unger, 1990). In supported education use is made of college campuses as settings to provide a comprehensive rehabilitation program for older adolescents and young adults. "The goal of the program is to assist students to choose a career goal and develop and implement a career plan so they may enter or re-enter the work force in the occupation of their choice.... Students learn career development skills while they attend classes" (p. 3). Examples of such programs may be found at Boston University, Buffalo State College, LaGuardia College of the City University of New York, and at George Brown College in Toronto, Canada.

Congress has been considering a number of proposals for reorganizing public education, including a federal mandate for setting national standards. If such a mandate were enacted into law, it would be the first time that the federal government became involved in the detail of curriculum building and testing, matters formerly left to the states and local school boards. Whether such standards would pose credentialing problems for students who are handicapped remains to be seen. Congress also has been discussing the benefits of setting up a number of demonstration schools and encouraging greater involvement of business and industry in secondary education. Will such new demonstrations, which are supposed to be complete reorganizations of school and education practice, incorporate any of the changes previously proposed for special education? Will the greater interest of the business community stretch to opening opportunities for handicapped youngsters through vocational education? These possibilities are discussed in the next chapter.

CHAPTER 5

THE WORLD OF WORK

When adolescents reach the age of 15 or 16, the question of what kind of work they will do in the future becomes increasingly important. The world of work, as it were, "has reared its ugly head." Adolescents aspire to adult roles, and earning money, if not actually a living, becomes an important goal. Much has been written about the value of work to the human being (see, for example, Neff, 1968; Hall, 1986; Black, 1988; Munich & Glinberg, 1988). It is sufficient to point out that in our culture, in addition to filling economic need, one's work is an identifier: It defines the role one plays in society. Work provides self-esteem as well as the esteem of others. We believe in the philosophy that "useful work and occupational self-sufficiency are important goals in life, that work not only facilitates emotional stability, but is also a source of happiness and satisfaction" (Hartmann et al., 1968, 178). For disabled persons work also represents another pattern of "normalization"; "it is a fundamental activity in a person's testing and strengthening of his sanity" (Munich & Glinberg, 1988, 121).

For young persons who have been mentally ill, a work setting can provide an acceptable structure for their time and abilities, as well as an opportunity to improve their skills in work tasks and interpersonal relations. As Herron (1981) explained in relation to runaway youngsters, "These young people, who have trouble liking and respecting themselves, are more prone to self-destructive behavior and to crises at home, in school, and with peers. One way to improve a young person's self-image and give him greater purpose and future goals is to provide employment and the support services necessary to keep him employed" (p. 103).

CAREER, VOCATION

An educational psychologist (Kuhlen 1952) pointed out a generation ago that "early vocational 'interests' reflect the maturation of general interest patterns; in early years they are fanciful, but by high school tend to reflect convention. Many job preferences in adolescence represent sheer fantasy; a large proportion of adolescents fail even to indicate a choice; and much evidence points to unrealism and ignorance in choice, in salary aspirations, and in plans for training. Need for realistic guidance is obvious" (p. 547). With regard to disabled youngsters, particularly the mentally ill, behaviorally disturbed, the situation has not changed. In a review of the experience of a consortium of schools offering vocational education to learning-disabled and behavior-disordered children (Dick, 1985), there was concern expressed that "the inadequate use of previous vocational assessment reports, reflected the special educators' lack of knowledge about how to interpret and use typical vocational assessment terminology and information" (p. 11).

Nevertheless, it is to the vocational area that the public

schools turn when they propose greater attention to preparation of youngsters for the world of work. The consortium of five schools just mentioned developed a four-phase program starting with a vocational evaluation using computerized testing equipment and including a simulated work environment. The process took 4 days for each child and was spread over 3 weeks. The evaluation was then used by counselors, special education teachers, and administrators in planning classroom instruction and placement decisions. A "transition objectives manual" was developed to classify a listing of career and vocational goals and objectives for the IEPs (see Chapter 3). Once the classroom instruction developed from the transition objectives manual had been completed, the students were to be ready for vocational training, and would be mainstreamed into the regular vocational and career education programs. The final phase, naturally, was to be placement and follow-up, hopefully to be "developed in cooperation with business and industry, post-secondary programs, and community agencies" (Dick, 1985, p.6).

Another example of a school program designed to assist high school students with vocational planning is reported in a handbook for rural school administrators and teachers (Feis & Werbel, 1983). Here, again, the program begins with a series of curriculum models to be used as alternative curricula in subject areas. The models are taught in resource rooms by a speech-language specialist, a counselor, and/or a vocational education teacher, depending on the subject and the students' disabilities. The didactic instruction is followed by a series of visits to the classroom by community employers and business leaders who inform the students about the work world in their areas; and this is followed by field visits to work sites in the community. For those students not planning on postsecondary education, an array of short work experiences are provided in the school buildings and in the community. Class credit is given for this experience, but there are no wages paid. Finally, part-time work can be obtained at the school or at community job sites, and for these there is pay at minimum wage as well as class credit.

What have become known as "alternative schools" have become popular where there are groups of children with special needs. Alternative high schools allow for a more flexible curriculum, often related to the employment opportunities in the surrounding community or to particular fields of endeavor. For example, the New York City Board of Education developed a linkage program with the New York City Housing Authority (The Benchmark, 1990). "Teachers, paraprofessionals, and community service aides, working cooperatively with tenant associations provide services such as instructional and vocational counseling, individualized programs, independent study courses, computer-assisted instruction, and the use of MetroGuide, a computer-based information system offering data about a wide array of educational and vocational programs" (p. 6).

An increasing number of school districts are turning to community-based rehabilitative agencies for assistance in vocational planning for students. Some are making use of the job preparation facilities of the federal job training program JTPA (Jobs Training Partnership Act). More will be said about these programs later in this chapter. A few school systems have invested in the equipment and personnel to provide their own vocational evaluations. (For a brief outline of the processes and equipment used in vocational evaluations, see Black, 1988.) I visited the special high school program operated by the New York City Board of Education in the psychiatry department of Bellevue Hospital. There, a complete battery of Singer Corporation computer-assisted work samples were used as part of the vocational testing and advising program. The difficulty was that the school could provide counseling and experience in only the very few work areas it was equipped to teach. Because of the nature of the student population, and the fact that the school had few contacts in the business or work world, there was almost no opportunity for students to consider or follow areas in which, according to the ornate vocational evaluation, they showed interest and possible proficiency.

It is interesting that in the experiential education programs mentioned in chapter 3 (Wehlage et al., 1982), two of the schools studied had strong vocational components. The authors reported that these "approached the concept of experiential education." "The primary differences between a work component and an experiential component," said their report, "is that the former tends to emphasize monetary rewards for the students, is more limited in the range of activities and roles a student can undertake, and is not as likely to stimulate reflection about social issues." Nonetheless, they reported, "The chance to get a job was one of the reasons cited by students for entering the program and accepting its rules and expectations" (pp. 185-186).

THE LAWS OF WORK FOR THE HANDICAPPED

Fair Labor Standards Act

The law that governs the conditions under which young persons, usually under 16 years of age, can be employed is the Fair Labor Standards Act of 1938, as amended. Under Section 14 of this act the Secretary of Labor is authorized to issue special certificates "in order to prevent curtailment of opportunities for employment" of persons "whose earning or productive capacity is impaired by age or physical or mental capacity" (pp. 101-157 Sect. 14). Special provision is made in the act for limited hours of part-time work for children in the 14- to 16-year age range. Each state has labor laws that either replicate the federal act or add restrictions as to age or allowed number of hours of work. Although exceptions to some of the child labor provisions are made to allow for school-supervised and school-administered work, career exploration programs, and student learner programs, restrictions are placed on the number of hours per day and week that minors under the age of 16 may work, and on the employment in hazardous occupations of children under the age of 18.

The Fair Labor Standards Act sets the national statutory minimum wage (at $4.25 an hour, as of April 1, 1991) and the provisions for paying wages to handicapped persons in sheltered workshops or work activity centers. In general, these are determined as a percentage of the prevailing wage for the occupation, but, with rare exceptions, not below 50% of the rate for a full-time nonhandicapped worker. It should be noted that since the amendments of 1966 and a decision of the U.S. Supreme Court, these wage and hour provisions apply also to "a hospital, an institution primarily engaged in the care of the sick, the aged, the mentally ill or defective who reside on the premises of such institution, a school for mentally or physically handicapped or gifted children . . ." (Dist. Col. 96 SCT 2465426 U.S. 1321). The Supreme Court decision, however, exempted employees of institutions operated by a state or local governmental agency. The amendments of 1989 added a provision that could have particular application to the transition of youngsters with disabilities from school to work:

Under certain conditions, employers may pay a training wage of at least 85 percent of the minimum wage for up to 90 days to employees under age 20, except for migrant or seasonal agricultural workers and for H-2A non-immigrant aliens performing agricultural work of a temporary or seasonal nature. An employee who has been paid at the training wage for 90 days can be employed for 90 additional days by a different employer, if that employer provides on-the-job training in accordance with regulations to be issued by the Secretary of Labor. Employers are prohibited from displacing regular employees in order to hire employees eligible for the training wage, and there is a limitation on the proportion of an employer's workforce which may receive the training wage. This provision expired March 31, 1993. (NARF, 1990a, pp. 1-2)

Targeted Jobs Tax Credit Program

One of the incentives for the employment of the handicapped has been use of the Targeted Jobs Tax Credit (TJTC), a provision of the U.S. Tax Reform Act of 1986. Under this provision, an employer may credit 40% of the first $6,000 in wages of a handicapped employee after an employment period of 90 days or 120 hours. Both the state departments of vocational rehabilitation and a number of rehabilitation ser-vice agencies have utilized the Targeted Jobs Tax Credit in convincing prospective employers to hire rehabilitees. There are limitations on the use of this tax credit for younger employees, and its greatest disadvantage is that it labels, and may stigmatize, persons so employed. In 1990 the TJTC was renewed (P.L. 101-508). Bills were introduced in both the House and the Senate of the U.S. Congress to permanently extend and expand the TJTC program (NARF, 1991a) but these were buried in a presidential veto of the onmibus tax bills of which they were part. At present there is an agreement between the appropriate committees of the Senate and the House to extend TJTC retroactively when Congress passes an extension (PSR Connection, 1992).

Projects with Industry

The Vocational Rehabilitation Act Amendments of 1968 (P.L. 90-391) authorized a program to provide more direct linkages between rehabilitation programs and the private business sector. It began as a small demonstration program and has grown to embrace 115 Projects With Industry (PWI) in fiscal year 1990, each receiving competitive grants through the U.S. Department of Education. Grantees include rehabilitation facilities, state departments of vocational rehabilitation, trade associations, and businesses working in conjunction with Business Advisory Councils appointed by the governor of the state and local officials.

Four models of Projects With Industry are available. Some of the grantees provide more than one model in their projects. The models are:

1. Job placement model. Places work-ready clients in competitive employment. Uses a "job coach" and a placement counselor. The Business Advisory Council does job development and monitors the job-seeking program.
2. Work adjustment model. Uses transitional worksites under the supervision of a rehabilitation counselor or "job coach." PWI staff maintain contact with the client

after placement to improve job-retention rates. The Business Advisory Council assists in the job placement of clients.

3. Skills training model. Uses classroom-instruction format for training at the rehabilitation facility or in industry. The Business Advisory Council oversees curriculum and job development, and helps in job placement after skills training.

4. Linkage model. Organizations in a geographical area work together in a network to expedite referrals, matching clients to jobs. There is a local advisory board of all participating businesses and rehabilitation facilities. Job openings within participating companies are listed at the project office, which notifies the rehabilitation agencies. (Black, 1988, p. 90; see also NARF, 1991a, p. 2)

The major use of PWI programs has been for persons with mental retardation or developmental disabilities. Examples of their use for youngsters with emotional handicaps will be given in the next chapter. Continuation of the PWI program nationally depends on the reauthorization of the Rehabilitation Act. This was passed by Congress and became law as P.L. 102-569, the Rehabilitation Act Amendments of 1992. PWI is included as Title VI and specifies that PWI "should address the career needs of individuals with disabilites" (NRA Newsletter, Dec. 1992).

The Rehabilitation Act and the Americans with Disabilities Act of 1990

As I pointed out in Chapter 3, these two pieces of legislation constitute a civil rights mandate for persons with disabilities. Section 504 of the Rehabilitation Act and Title I of the Americans with Disabilities Act (P.L. 101-336) cover discrimination in employment. As the National Association of Rehabilitation Facilities asserts (NARF, 1991b):

> The new law [Americans With Disabilities Act] is expected to help in removing barriers to employment and public entities, which have often made persons with disabilities less than fully participating and accepted members of our society. In addition the new law will provide an opportunity for facilities to work with and educate the business community on the needs of persons with disabilities, how to make places of business successful, and the rights of persons with disabilities. (p.3)

Job Training Partnership Act

Federal manpower training programs have been part of the national scene since the days of the Roosevelt administration in the 1930s. Primarily designed for the alleviation of poverty, they linked ideas of training and education to meet the needs of workers displaced through changing technology and/or economic conditions. They have also emphasized programs for youth. The manpower training programs have over the years made only occasional mention of services to the handicapped. The latest of the national programs, the Job Training Partnership Act (P.L. 97-300) simply specifies (Section 203-2) that "up to 10 percent of the participants in a service delivery area receiving assistance under this part may be individuals who are not economically disadvantaged if such individuals have encountered barriers to employment." The word "handicapped" is included in the list that follows.

The Job Training Partnership Act differs from its predecessor manpower training ventures in centering control in the states instead of in the national administration. Each governor divides the state into Service Delivery Areas (SDAs) and appoints local Private Industry Councils (PICs) to train and place people into jobs. There are also some federally administered programs, for example, Job Corps, veterans' employment, and national programs that cannot effectively be done by the states. These latter provide for people who are disabled, persons receiving public assistance, legal offenders, and other special interest groups. However, the national programs are restricted to a small proportion of the total fiscal appropriations made available. The legislation originating the JTPA was introduced in Congress in 1982 by then Senator Dan Quayle.

JTPA mandates that the PICs expend 40% of their annual funding on youth (Section 203b-2). A study by the National Commission for Employment Policy (Sandell 1988) reported that while youth constituted 17.8% of the eligible population, they constituted over 40% of all participants. This report concluded, "The JTPA system is successfully emphasizing services to youth. . . . Youth dropouts display a relatively high participation rate, especially those who are unemployed. More than 28 percent of eligible unemployed youth dropouts are served by JTPA programs" (p. 73).

In contrast, the United States General Accounting Office, an arm of Congress, reported to the chairmen of the concerned committees of the House and Senate on a study of a random sample of 5,000 youth from a nationally representative sample of 63 local JTPA programs as follows:

> A comparison of the JTPA out-of-school youth sample and the eligible population indicates that there is little targeting of services to those with greatest need—the less job ready. But there is also little evidence that JTPA is "creaming" by serving a disproportionately high number of those who have less need—the more job ready. . . . About half of the out-of school JTPA youth participants received occupational training, a majority of which was for moderate or higher skill occupations. A fourth of the out-of-school youth received nonoccupational training, and about a fifth got job search assistance only. . . . Certain groups of youth, particularly the less job ready, those aged 15 to 17, dropouts, and black males, were less likely to get moderate or higher skill occupational training than the average for all participants. Nonoccupational training may be the more appropriate assistance for dropouts. As with adults, youth, particularly the more job ready, were often given on-the-job training in lower skill jobs for periods exceeding the length of time usually required for such jobs. (GAO, 1991, pp. 20-23)

Job search assistance is usually the shortest in duration. It consists of short-term counseling and training in how to look for employment. Nonoccupational training is generally composed of low-skilled training focused on work attitudes and behavior.

In a comment prescient to this book the GAO stated: "Dropouts may be in a position to benefit more from occupational training when it is accompanied by either remedial education or participation in exemplary youth programs. About 2 percent of all out-of-school youth were enrolled in either exemplary youth programs or remedial education and also in occupational training" (p. 28).

The leading criticisms of JTPA, as recounted in newspaper articles and in a report of the Inspector General of the U.S. Department of Labor are as follows:

Nearly 50% of JTPA enrollees were not on the job for which they were trained just 4 months after completing their training.

JTPA supplies misleading figures on success, in that the program supplies follow-up for only 3 months after training.

JTPA does not place people in good jobs. Nearly two thirds of out-of-school youth are placed in jobs at wages only slightly more than the minimum wage.

There is a strong feeling (shared in by independent governmental agencies) that a majority of employers would have hired individuals for jobs for which they received salary subsidies—with or without JTPA's funding help.

The program, in the words of one newspaper, is "a 3.7 billion dollar annual boondoggle" (*Times Union*, 1988). On the other hand, JTPA supporters insist that without the private sector involvement the program would not work. The vice president of a food distribution company stated to the *Times Union*, "JTPA helps us immensely. A training period is extremely costly to a company. The fact that the government will participate in the education . . . enables us to hire people who may have no grocery experience already" (*Times Union*, Business Section, p. 1). It should be noted that state governments are increasingly using JTPA as an economic development tool to keep a company in an area or attract a new firm.

In spite of the criticisms and the ostensible limitations in the program, particularly for youth, I reiterate the conclusion I reached in 1987 (Black, 1988) that JTPA can be of great help in the transition of mentally ill and emotionally disturbed youngsters into the world of work. A number of rehabilitation agencies have found participation in JTPA valuable, as I shall describe in the next chapter. It is important to keep in mind that others may also find it possible to use this manpower training program, and, if past practice is repeated, there can be modifications to law or regulations making the eligibility of the handicapped more feasible. The Job Training Partnership Act was reauthorized and signed into law in September 1992 for another 5 years as P.L. 102-367. These amendments "targeted 65 percent of the training and employment resources to individuals who are hard-to-serve as well as economically disadvantaged. Persons with disabilities . . . are included in the hard-to-serve category" (PSR Connection, December 1992, p. 3).

PROS AND CONS OF WORK FOR TEENAGERS

Our culture looks with favor on youngsters having jobs, after school, during holidays, and between high school and college, or further vocational training. It is assumed that such work experience will teach the value of money and the adult responsibilities of working with others and under supervision. It is also expected that the youngsters will gain a greater stake in the world of business and industry in making an adult contribution to the gross national product. In other terms, such part-time or interim work is thought to aid in the development of a "work personality" (see Black, 1988, p. 43). One has in mind a picture of a youngster delivering newspapers, serving behind a grocery counter, delivering for a pharmacy, or the like.

The authors of the study *When Teenagers Work* (Friedenberg, 1987) challenge this conventional wisdom. They maintain that the circumstances under which teenagers are employed are much different from those of adults and that "part-time jobs held by adolescents provide very little opportunity for the kind of socialization into the world of work that parents foresee as beneficial" (p. 4). Nearly two thirds of high school seniors are employed, and in 1986 they were earning on average about $275 per month for 20 hours per week.

These authors contend that "neither the jobs nor the work settings available to American adolescents today can serve as transitions to adulthood. Adolescent experience is seldom broadened by the kind of work adolescents actually do. Instead, their work becomes an impoverished and driven extension of their life in the peer-culture. Most of the money they earn goes to support teenage tastes, addictions, and patterns of conspicuous consumption." The assumption is that most teenagers are employed in such fast-food outlets as McDonalds and Kentucky Fried Chicken and that, employed there, the youngsters are forfeiting "their opportunities for genuine maturation by giving up their leisure and the chances it might have afforded them for reflection—including the daydreaming and goofing off required by the growing sense of self—and for really involving themselves with other people in sports, clubs, and service they themselves recognize as valuable to the community" (p. 4). The authors emphasize that such employment tends to debase their understanding of the value of money because it makes them "irresponsibly affluent and therefore selfish."

Although this point of view may have some merit, it overglamorizes the earlier work opportunities for teenagers in general, and assumes that because earnings are used for what teenagers desire they are not validly used. As for the youngsters we are concerned with here, the mentally ill and emotionally disturbed, the opportunities in part-time work, if the student is capable of maintaining it, far outweigh any theoretical values for them in "goofing off" and daydreaming. I do not see any less value in work behind a counter in a fast-food establishment than that in a structured sheltered workshop, for example, as utilized by rehabilitation agencies in developing the "work personality."

THE CHANGING SCENE OF WORK

What kind of a work world will the youngsters, including our mentally ill, emotionally disturbed, and behaviorally disordered, graduate into? The opinions of economists, business leaders, and union chiefs paint a rapidly changing scene—one that, depending on one's view, can be either devastating or a window of opportunity for those who are disabled.

The U.S. Commissioner of Labor Statistics (*Science Focus*, 1988) summed up the picture: "Dramatic structural changes in the American work force have taken place in the 1980s, brought on by the rapid implacement of new technologies, particularly in professional, managerial, and technical areas of employment" (pp. 1, 12). He pointed out that in 1987 the number of white-collar employees in the labor force equaled, for the first time, the number of blue-collar workers. According to the New York State Commissioner of Labor (Hartnett,

1990), "We are steadily becoming a service-oriented economy.
. . . That means most people will work in information gathering/manipulation, or health care, or repair fields, not on the assembly lines. Americans might still build a better mousetrap, but more of us than ever before will be employed in supplying the cheese and emptying the traps" (p. 1).

The president of the New York State AFL-CIO (Cleary, 1990) declared, "We must . . . use highly skilled and trained workers operating the world's most sophisticated technology" (p. 3). However, as *Business Week* (1988) pointed out, "More than three-quarters of the nation's new workers will have limited verbal and writing skills. But they will be competing for only 10% of the new jobs. Most new jobs will require workers who have solid reading and writing skills, but fewer than one in four new employees will be able to function at the needed levels" (p. 104). The young people who are subjects of this book will for the most part be numbered among the latter.

While the U.S. Department of Labor's Bureau of Labor Statistics reports that the fastest growing occupations in our economy are mainly in the health-related areas (*The Benchmark*, 1990), the occupations which will have the largest job growth by the year 2000 include such lower skilled jobs as retail salespersons; janitors and cleaners; waitresses and waiters; general office clerks; secretaries; nursing aides, orderlies, and attendants; truck drivers, and receptionists. This leads to another, more promising viewpoint for the transition of disabled young people from school to work. "The media have put an enormous emphasis on high tech jobs in terms of the *percentage* of growth. . . . As a result of this kind of hype, the Education Commission of the States . . . said that every high school graduate would have to have a set of very sophisticated skills in order to get any job in an increasingly high tech world" (Hodgkinson, 1986, p. 8). Speaking for the National

Center for Research in Vocational Education, Hodgkinson goes on to say:

> We turn out six nontechnical jobs for every one remotely connected with high technology. . . . We are talking about 500,000 cashiers' jobs every year. We are simply not going to need 500,000 fibre optic specialists in the next few years. . . . I feel that most will not need high level skills in order to get a job because as a janitor or a truck driver they simply won't be necessary. However, skills such as the ability to make decisions, to think logically or to communicate clearly are certainly valuable for citizenship. (p.8)

As the Grant Commission (Legislative Brief, 1988) phrased it, "After all, chefs, plumbers, electricians, carpenters, machinists, pipe fitters, masons, welders, diesel mechanics, and medical and dental technicians—already in short supply—are occupations likely to provide far more employment, often at far better wages, than the highly-touted high tech jobs" (p. 3).

On the one hand, then, is the opinion that increasing technology is requiring that "workers and repair technicians must be able to process information *symbolically* which requires not only higher literacy skills to read complicated manuals and diagrams, but the ability to think and reason differently" (Cole, 1989, p. 4). On the other hand is the opinion that only a small proportion of the new jobs will require higher basic education, and that for most entry-level positions the basic reading, writing, and arithmetic will more than suffice. Even if the latter turns out to be true, the problem still remains of providing this amount of education to youngsters who have interrupted or truncated schooling.

Interestingly, while the business community complains about the inadequacies of the school systems and the lack of preparedness of the people it seeks to employ, it seems to be coming to the conclusion that specialized training for the job skills required will largely have to be given by the business or industry itself with or without the participation of the public schools. This would appear to agree with the point of view of educators, as illustrated in the response of the Chancellor of the New York City School System (Letter, 1990) to a query from his Advisory Council for Occupational Education:

> The primary mission of a public high school is to provide students with a basic academic experience that permits them to select from among a full range of career and academic options. Our goal is to guarantee that every graduate has sufficient preparation to choose whether college or an occupation. We are not a training facility for private industry; we are an educational institution. Occupational education programs should function as a life option to which students are exposed, but not as a track to which they are channeled. (p. 1)

The Grant Commission report (U.S. Department of Labor, 1989) states that "on-the-job training, broadly defined, provides the most direct route to useful employment that our economic system can offer to those who are not headed for full-time post-secondary education" (p. 39). This is particularly important in meeting the demands of the new technologies, for, as the New York Academy of Sciences points out (Science Focus, 1988,) "in almost every industry where new technology has been introduced in recent decades, workers have been required to learn new skills" (p. 1).

The impetus that this can give to apprenticeship training should be obvious. Its relationship to the concept of "experiential learning" should also be clear. Together, as we shall see in the next chapter, they comprise important elements in the programs needed for assisting mentally ill young people make the transition to the world of work. The U.S. Department of Labor indicates that at present there are about 400 school-to-apprenticeship programs, involving some 1,500 high school students, most of them initiated in the 1970s as pilot programs. The earlier federal manpower training ventures, CETA (Comprehensive Employment and Training Act) and the Job Corps, did have programs linking apprenticeship with services to disadvantaged youth, but the current JTPA has not replicated these on any widespread basis. Hopefully, revisions in the law, now being considered in Congress, will modify this.

A WINDOW OF OPPORTUNITY?

There are many rehabilitation specialists who look upon the next decade as opening a window of opportunity for employment of the disabled. The decline in the numbers of new entrants into the labor market as the baby boom population has passed its peak, and as immigration to the United States has been tightened, forces business and industry to turn to population groups ignored in the past—minorities, the economically and socially disadvantaged, the disabled. The trend to technology can open the door for those with handicaps who can master sufficient education to fill the positions in technical occupations. There should be many opportunities in job areas that really do not require advanced education for their performance.

In addition, "many vocational rehabilitation personnel," says Paul Cornes (1987), "are optimistic about the potential of new technology because new jobs created by microtechnology, in which physical requirements are replaced by electronic skill, strength and precision, may be particularly suitable for people with disabilities and because new developments in communications should increase opportunities for home-based employment." Cornes points out, however, that "there are reasons why such optimism may need to be qualified." First of all, many persons who are disabled may not have the level of education to benefit from training in the new fields. Then, "the planning, communication and teamwork skills necessary for such jobs all require personal qualities, like confidence and independence, which are rarely enhanced in a disabled person's life experience" (p. 5).

Forecasting economic trends is always risky. Rehabilitation specialists may be too optimistic about there being a window of opportunity; certain economists may be overly pessimistic in predicting a lessened need for employees altogether (especially persons with handicaps) as technology takes over from personnel. It seems to me, however, that there will no doubt be a middle ground, where, with the proper combination of supports from education, rehabilitation, and business and industry, the young people with whom this book is concerned can find their niche in the world of work. It is hard for me to believe that many troubled young folk who are quite able to master Nintendo and Star Wars games cannot learn to cope with the entry-level basics of a technological job world.

SUBSTITUTE PERMANENT AND TRANSITIONAL EMPLOYMENT

Throughout this century, use has been made of work settings

that are facsimiles of the real thing to provide service to people who are handicapped and who are not able or not acceptable to work in normal business and industry. The oldest of these has been the sheltered workshop, usually a bench-assembly or semiskilled industry, under nonprofit sponsorship, accepting simple work tasks under contract with regular industry. In some instances the sheltered workshop undertakes direct manufacturing of products for sale. While some nonhandicapped personnel may be employed in a sheltered workshop, generally in supervisory positions or for special operations requiring additional skills, the majority of employees are persons with handicaps who received wages related to their productivity, under special provisions of the federal and state wage and hour labor laws (for a more complete description of sheltered workshops, see Black, 1988, and Nelson, 1971).

Sheltered workshops are most familiar to the public as industries for the blind, or as those serving the severely mentally retarded. In an earlier era, sheltered workshops were used for employees of industry who were recovering from tuberculosis but were still too infectious to return to their regular trades. Sheltered workshops were also a source of employment for persons who were confined to wheelchairs because of accident or illness or who were otherwise restricted by prostheses. In those times such persons were considered unable to work again in normal industry. Although some use was made of sheltered workshops for training or retraining, as transition to competitive employment, they most usually became what economists referred to as "substitute permanent employment."

When sheltered workshops began to be used for dischargees

from mental hospitals, in the 1950s and 1960s (Black, 1988), it was expected that they would be temporary havens until the ex- patients gained skills and confidence and, like the tuberculosis patients before them, would enter or return to regular employment. However, experience showed that the numbers of such transits from sheltered to open employment were small; sheltered employment became extended and often permanent employment.

Led by the Fountain House Foundation in New York City, a "psychosocial club" for ex-mental patients, the mental health field borrowed a British formula and turned directly to private industry for work training and experience—the "transitional employment program" (TEP) was developed. In this program, a business would agree to hold an entry-level job open as a TEP to be filled by clients of the mental health agency. For example, a department store might make available a stock-clerk position to be filled by two clients, each half time. A staff member of the agency would learn the procedures of the job, to teach them to the clients and to guarantee that the work would be done to the satisfaction of the employer if for any reason clients were unavailable or nonperforming. Regular wages are paid by the employer for hours worked, directly to the clients in the original Fountain House plan or, in variations on the plan, to the mental health agency, which in turn paid the clients. (For a more complete description see Black, 1988, and Beard, 1976.) The mental health services are responsible for costs of supervision and of supportive services and treatment required. The job sites are considered strictly training sites, and, except for one of the many variations of the TEP model, did not become places of permanent employment for any client.

There are no economic gains for an employer to participate in a TEP, except the guarantee that one job slot would be regularly filled and the possibility of access to potential new employees (for other job slots) who have demonstrated ability in the work. The employer's contribution to helping meet one of society's needs is great. As I shall show in the next chapter, the linkage of TEP with secondary education is one way to provide very promising elements in an approach to meeting the transition needs of mentally ill youngsters graduating from school to work.

SUPPORTED WORK

The latest approach in a transition to open competitive employment is "supported work." The term "supported work" was coined "in the early 1980s, when advocates and service providers for persons with mental retardation became increasingly aware that special education students were not making the transition from high school to the competitive labor force . . . there were few jobs available for special education graduates, and few adult services that afforded anything more than segregated custodial care" (Anthony & Blanch, 1987, p. 7). In passing the 1984 amendments to the Education for the Handicapped Act (P.L. 98-199), Congress noted the lack of transitional services for students from special education. The Developmental Disabilities Act of 1984 (P.L. 98-527) included a mandate for "employment-related" activities, specifically identifying "supported employment." In 1986, Congress passed amendments to the Rehabilitation Act of 1973 (P.L. 99-506), which included supported employment as well as transitional employment services as fundable activities, and included persons with psychiatric disabilities among those eligible. These have been continued in Title IV of the Rehabilitation Act Amendments of 1992.

According to the 1986 Rehabilitation Act Amendments, supported employment is competitive work in integrated settings, work sites where there are nonhandicapped as well as handicapped employees. "Supported employment focuses on employment and training in actual jobs rather than preparation for employment. It uses a place/train as opposed to a train/place approach. The individual is placed in an appropriate job and then provided with intense training on the job site in job skills and work related behaviors. Most training is provided at the job site although certain job related skills may require instruction in other locations (e.g., travel training on city buses)" (President's Committee, 1990, p. 1).

In the last few years there has been increasing interest in tailoring supported employment programs for persons with psychiatric disabilities. For example, Fabian and Wiedefeld (1989) describe the S.T.E.P. model (Schapiro Training and Employment Program):

> Individuals are placed directly into integrated competitive settings working for real wages an average of 20 hours per week. . . . At placement, the job coach works with the employee for as long as necessary to insure job stability and maintenance. . . . Job coaches focus on interpersonal skill development, including modelling appropriate social interactions with co-workers and supervisors. . . . Although this population may acquire adequate job skills more quickly

than developmentally disabled persons, production is often
well below employer expectations, requiring intervention
strategies to increase production rate. As the employee
begins to function more independently on the job, the coach
systematically fades out of the work environment. (p. 60)

It is significant to note that the emphasis on "integrated"
work environments stems from the same philosophy as "least
restrictive environment" in the education laws (see Chapter 3).
Also, the place/train idea has connotations parallel to experiential and hands on learning in the field of education and to on-
the-job training and apprenticeship from the fields of labor
and manpower training. Although there is reference to the
source of wages, as in, "Supported employment programs . .
. move from referral and assessment directly to job placement,
with the company generally paying the wages and the agency
providing the supervision and support," there is almost nothing said about the tasks and procedures for acquiring supported work sites or the actual relations between employers
and agencies.

The experience to date with supported work for persons
with psychiatric disabilities has raised several issues. The role
and responsibilities of the job coach have come under scru-
tiny. Instead of a "fading out," as in services to the developmentally disabled and in the S.T.E.P. example above, perhaps
the nature of psychiatric disability requires a series of inter-
mittent peaks and drop offs (Fabian & Wiedefeld, 1989). At
the same time, agencies experienced with clients who have a
variety of disabilities are reporting that changes are taking
place in the roles of the job coaches (also referred to as site
managers and as employment specialists). They are assuming

more of the responsibilities formerly reserved for central staff, including those of rehabilitation managers and market managers (NARF, 1988). There are also questions being raised as to the specific training and skills required of job coaches to enable them to work with persons who are psychiatrically disabled.

Another issue has to do with the kinds of jobs available through supported employment. Fabian and Wiedefeld (1989) pointed out that entry-level jobs with little future advancement may not fit the needs of the psychiatrically disabled population. They state:

> The supported employment model . . . with its emphasis on the job coach serving as the employment trainer, implies that in order to assure that the staff member can perform this role, jobs must be simple enough for that individual to learn in a couple of days or perhaps a week. Alternatively, it may be that in this model, the job coach should not be the job trainer, but rather the job supporter, thus allowing increasingly complex jobs to be sought matching the skill level of the prospective employee without requiring that each job coach be an occupational expert. (p. 58)

At the insistence of the mental health service providers, the law and regulations for the amendments to the Rehabilitation Act (P.L. 99-506) define transitional employment programs for the psychiatrically disabled as a form of supported employment, thus making them eligible for vocational rehabilitation funding. While there are many similarities, the obvious difference between TEP and supported employment is that the former is most usually temporary work and the latter is intended to be regular continued employment.

Unions have shown a good deal of interest in the supported employment model. They have long taken a dim view of sheltered workshops, because some workshops have continued to perform contract work with employers whose own employees have been out on strike, and because they often accept work from nonunion plants that are in competition with unionized ones. As one labor union official commented, "Rather than working people with disabilities into regular jobs through attrition and through openings, employers have replaced bargaining units by contracting out the work. That's left a very bad taste in the mouths of some people" (p. 10). The unions' position is that subcontracting means that union members lose their jobs and the union loses members. They add, "For people with disabilities the value of working in unionized jobs stems from the opportunity to be part of society, to be integrated rather than segregated" (Unions, 1990, p. 10).

There is an underlying philosophy to supported work that is sometimes implied in transitional and substitute employment, but never made so objective. Anthony and Blanch (1987) state it clearly: "The supported employment approach, in contrast [to earlier concepts of disability] assumes that all people— regardless of the severity of their disability—can do meaningful, productive work in normal settings, if that is what they choose to do, and if they are given the necessary supports. Failures are due not to the disability itself but to inappropriate job selection or to inadequate supports" (p. 7).

It would appear that with the Americans With Disabilities Act before us and congressional reauthorization of the Rehabilitation Act with its Section 504 having just been completed there should be tremendous impetus for making this philosophy a reality. As we shall see later in this chapter, however, there is a countering philosophy with a longer history, and many barriers must be overcome before any window of opportunity in the job employment world can be really accessible.

TO WORK OR NOT TO WORK

Our society is faced with two underlying philosophies of treatment of the ill or handicapped, which may appear contradictory. On the one hand, we express concern and sympathy for the deserving disabled through charity and, since the great Depression of the 1930s, with governmentally funded income maintenance schemes. These have the effect of providing for the necessities of life without expecting or requiring the recipients to work. On the other, we are increasingly emphasizing the rights and responsibilities of handicapped individuals to "normalize," to enter or reenter the labor market and make a contribution to the gross national product. Lamb (1987) expresses this dilemma for the seriously psychiatrically ill:

> How does this [the value of vocational rehabilitation] square with a system in which continued financial support at a low standard of living is contingent upon the patient maintaining a sick status? When one includes Medicaid, food stamps, the supplement to the basic federal grant supplied by a number of states, exemption from income taxes, and the possibility of pooling one's resources and living together with another recipient, the standard of living may not be so low. It is not surprising that a large percentage of the mentally ill remain "disabled" and totally (or almost

so) dependent on SSI. (p. 346)

A key word in the first philosophy is "deserving." As Brodsky (1987) explains, "There are . . . certain community criteria for the label of 'deserving' disabled. A man must be 'clean' (including his body, family, and house) and 'nice' (be friendly and sober and attend church), must not be idle, and must obtain a medical certification of disability that validates the disabled role and qualifies him for disability compensation" (p. 52). It is obvious that but few of the persons with psychiatric disabilities are likely to meet these criteria. Nevertheless, more and more of those persons with labeled psychiatric disabilities have been helped by mental health and other professionals to qualify for Social Security Disability (SSDI) and Social Security Supplemental Insurance (SSI) benefits, aided greatly in recent years by movements toward equal opportunities and by parents' groups and by advocacy by disabled people themselves.

In a review of the employment of persons with disabilities in the member states of the European Community (OECD, 1990), the ministers and others who participated concluded that:

> while the rights to education, training, and independent and small group living have been recognized, the right to employment in the community with others has been less often accorded. . . . Rights and opportunities are closely linked with professional expectations. Some professional groups have a vested interest in the separate dependent "handicap industry" while others have been at the forefront of new initiatives to support integration, independent living and employment. (p. 14)

Lamb (1987) adds the note that "mental health professionals often contribute to the problems. We are frequently reluctant to see our patients take low-status, minimum-wage jobs even though this is the present limit of their capabilities" (p. 348).

In the OECD (1990) review, it was decided that "the objectives for young people are seldom seen as appropriate for those who are disabled. If they are applied to those with disabilities there are usually explicit or implicit professional reservations about the future of individuals. Specific kinds and degrees of disability are often associated with stereotypical views of the future" (p. 10). According to Noble and Collignon (1987), the stereotypes that even well-meaning educational, social service, and mental health professionals apply to mental illness include the following:

Severe mental illness is a static condition.

Independent living is not feasible.

"Normalization" of lifestyle is not achievable.

Dangerousness is always a real possibility.

The constitutional right to liberty and freedom does not apply to individuals who are mentally ill because they cannot distinguish right from wrong, reality from hallucinations, and so forth. (p. 33)

We are inclined to forget that the stigma of mental illness is rooted in fear that has been part of our civilization for centuries. As I have said elsewhere:

We Westerners may not think of demons or other extrasensory explanations, as is common in Asia or Africa, but the man on the street and the worker in the work place often perceive the mentally ill as "raving lunatics," at worst as highly dangerous people who need to be locked up, and at least as people to be avoided. Vocational rehabilitation counselors have long advised clients to explain periods of absence from work as due to "nervous breakdowns" or some other euphemism rather than admit to psychiatric hospitalization. (Black, 1988, pp. 168-169)

It is understandable, then, why many persons who have had treatment for mental illness prefer not to approach or reapproach the world of work with the label of psychiatric disability. It is possible then, also, that a great disservice may be given youth so labeled in the school system, even if by so doing the extra provisions of education for the handicapped are made available.

Young people with emotional illnesses or behavioral disorders may be caught in yet another bind. The current emphasis in educational policy, federally and in a rapidly increasing number of states, is toward setting higher competency standards for high school graduation. In so doing, there is little if any provision for providing the tutorial or remedial assistance for the youngsters who fail the competency examinations the first time around. I would agree with Harold Hodgkinson (1986), who says,

If we're excluding people from high school graduation, it automatically means in the minds of some people that the standards are going up. Others have said that if we really wanted to raise test scores in schools we would simply kick out the handicapped kids and kids from low socioeconomic backgrounds. I find that not only disquieting, but somehow un-American. I find this attitude across political parties. This is particularly disconcerting now that we've discovered that programs such as Head Start have helped students considerably. (p. 5)

Fortunately, I believe there is enough advocacy for the disabled in our country today to ensure that the kinds of integrated programs I will discuss next will have sufficient support to demonstrate that many troubled youngsters can be helped to make adequate transitions from adolescence to adulthood and from school to work.

CHAPTER 6

TOWARD SUCCESSFUL
TRANSITIONS

Over recent years the Centre for Educational Research and
Innovation of the International Organisation for Economic
Cooperation and Development has been examining the programs for transition of disabled youngsters from school to
work in Western society. In a report entitled "The Road to
Adulthood," the Centre (OECD, 1990) defined transition as
"the process by which an individual grows through adolescence to adulthood in the social, cultural, economic and legal
contexts provided by families, communities and national
policies" (p. 6). The report goes on to say:

> Stated simply, the transition period has been recognized as
> increasingly important, particularly if all the resources
> devoted to early childhood programmes and to the educa-
> tion of those with disabilities and difficulties are to be used
> effectively. Transition to adulthood is a necessary phase in

a community's responsibility for the care and education of its young people. To neglect this phase, leave it to chance or to the vagaries of a chaotic non-system of different responsibilities is to be wasteful and neglectful. Neglect increases the long-term burden on society of those deemed handicapped. Appropriate transition programmes will increase the number of handicapped persons who can escape dependency and passivity and contribute and participate in society. (pp. 6-7)

How to achieve such a transition for young people who are mentally ill is the theme of this book. As we have seen, the process is complicated by the nature of the disability, the kinds and availability of schooling, the conditions of the world of work, the attitudes toward the illness, as well as by the organizational and administrative difficulties in putting a program together. As Modrcin (1988) puts it:

The concept of transition as it relates to adolescents can be viewed from two distinct perspectives. First, from a developmental perspective, adolescents are experiencing an identity crisis in their attempt to decide where they fit in society (separating from family, deciding on a career path, defining self, etc.). Second, from a situational or contextual perspective, adolescents must move from the world of school to the world of work and/or initiate more independent behavior in a variety of settings (maintaining a job, living on their own, etc.). Seriously emotionally handicapped adolescents represent a population group that will have difficulty coping with both developmental and situational transitions. Their behavior, the debilitating effect of the illness process, financial hardships, family stress, the lack of developed coping and social skills, and the lack of vocational skills or options for employment create barriers which make the adjustment to various transitions extremely difficult. (pp. 1-2)

Koroloff (1990) summarizes what educational experts consider the nine components of an adequate transition policy for youth with serious emotional disabilities. These are the following:

1. There must be a strong mechanism for interagency planning and coordination at the local level.
2. Adult-serving agencies must be involved prior to the time the youth leaves the child serving system.
3. There must be a process for identifying or initiating transition planning for the child at an early age.
4. The process for initiating transition planning should be automatic and not dependent on a unique request for each individual youth.
5. A variety of settings should serve as the point of identification and initiation of transition planning.
6. A person or system must be identified to take responsibility for planning and delivering services over a period of time, specifically past the age at which the youth must leave special education.
7. Parents and youth should be explicitly included in the planning and implementation of the transition process.
8. There must be an interdepartmental mechanism at the state level for the planning and coordination of services, as well as resolution of disputes.
9. The concept of transition services must be broadly construed to include all aspects of successful independent living. (p. 81)

It should not be surprising that the Centre for Educational Research and Innovation should come to recommend practically these same components as goals for services to all young people who are disabled. (OECD, 1990, p. 76). However, the Centre stressed one goal that I believe is especially crucial for successful transitional services for those who are mentally ill or emotionally disturbed: "The key message of this report is that young people with disabilities need a continuity of support if they are to make a successful transition to adult life. It is crucial that departments, agencies and professionals work to agreed ends to provide this continuity so that independence in working life can be achieved by all" (p. 77).

What is sometimes forgotten in planning services for people who have psychiatric disabilities is that the resulting handicaps do not remain constant. While treatment and attention to skill- learning and special and vocational education can increase the person's functioning capability, the exacerbating relapsing nature of the illness itself can have an opposing effect. Stability in functioning can be achieved, but only if there is constancy and continuity in services over time.

COOPERATIVE AGENCY AGREEMENTS

Shortly after the passage of P.L. 94-142 many states, recognizing that the provision of "related services" under the law required collaboration with other human service agencies, set about forging cooperative agreements. Generally, these included the state education department, its divisions of special and vocational education, and the state office of vocational rehabilitation. In many instances there was inclusion of departments of mental health, departments of mental retardation/developmental disabilities, and sometimes agencies for welfare and human services. The aim was to set a framework that local school districts could follow. "Most typically, the state educational authorities seek to promote joint local efforts around groups of handicapped children who require a rich mix of services" (Rogers & Farrow, 1983, p. 47).

For example, to meet the needs of handicapped youth, the education department of the state of Michigan developed an interagency agreement between its divisions of special and vocational education and the State Division of Rehabilitation Services; California developed an agreement between its education department and the Department of Mental Health; Oklahoma's agreement was between its education agency, its division of vocational education, and its agency for vocational rehabilitation. Rhode Island's education agency "recognized that services to severely handicapped children with behavioral disorders were in short supply statewide and that merely 'encouraging' local programs had not resulted in much new funding" (pp. 48-49). The education agency was "also interested in decreasing the number of expensive day and residential out-of-district placements for this group of children" (pp. 50-51). The state education agency solicited local applications for joint proposals between educational authorities and community mental health centers. Three-year demonstration projects were awarded to one county and two cities.

From experience with these agreements and those of other states, Rogers and Farrow (1983) extracted "common factors contributing to the effectiveness of interagency collaboration strategies." In brief, these were:

1. Involvement by the governor's office or even a resolution or an act by the state legislature would be most

helpful in ensuring the drafting and application of an interagency agreement.

2. The state must view its action as part of an ongoing process rather than as a one-time effort.

3. The participants in the agreement must be ready to commit resources, and particularly staff allocation, on a long-term basis; otherwise, little progress can be made.

4. Interagency efforts require firm leadership and direction.

5. The most successful strategies are those directed to a specific task, such as communication, problem solving, information sharing, or "deliberating on broad policy directions that state agencies must jointly establish and pursue" (p. 63).

6. The "informal dimensions," the relationships people on interagency committees establish, are often crucial for the success or failure of the effort.

7. The interagency efforts should seek to strengthen and formalize existing state linkages rather than create new ones.

8. Interagency collaboration should begin with a limited scope and expand into other areas only when the participants are comfortable with the outcome of the initial activities.

9. Interagency efforts at the state level are meaningless if there is no local implementation.

10. The most effective activities result when a forum for problem solving is provided in which each member of the interagency committees can participate.

Although descriptions of efforts at interagency agreements are heartening and seem to portend better and greater services to youngsters who are handicapped, they have not fulfilled their promises. As Tindall (1981) pointed out, "The process of forming even one linkage agreement can often be an extremely long one.... In many cases, there are already existing linkage agreements between departments at the state level. However, they do not always filter down to the local level" (p. 103). In 1985, Wehman and his colleagues concluded:

> Previous efforts at interagency agreements which purported to ameliorate transition problems actually resulted, in all too many cases, in movement of a student from one inadequate school program to another inadequate adult program. (p. 27)

> Unfortunately, efforts to encourage interagency cooperation have had little impact on the design and delivery of services. Although approximately 35 states have developed formal interagency agreements, and many communities have implemented local agreements, numerous problems persist. Agencies differ widely in their diagnostic terminology and eligibility criteria. Services continue to be duplicated, while communities fail to initiate programs (for example, supported work placement) which are needed to complete a local continuum of services. Political and attitudinal barriers also inhibit interagency cooperation. Administrators often enter collaborative efforts suspicious of the intentions of other agencies, defensive of their own "turf", and fearful that interagency cooperation may lead to budget cuts and termination of programs. (p. 31)

Gartner (1986, p. 179) adds, "A further complication in planning comes when it crosses what may be called institutional 'cultural' lines. . . . Institutions not only have different roles, they have different customs, ways of doing things, rhythms, mores, styles, indeed different 'bottom' lines. . . .A person whose experience has been in one setting may not easily make the transition to another, be it different in terms of sector, level, population served. Good utility infielders are hard to find."

By 1987, Friedman and Duchnowski had decided that "the status of interagency collaborations has been reviewed by several groups. The consensus appears to be on the one hand a recognition of the critical need for such efforts, but on the other hand a concern that the obstacles to effective collaboration efforts are so imposing that they can serve as an insurmountable barrier for all but the most dedicated groups" (pp. 2-3). Most recently, the Bank Street College of Education study (Knitzer et al., 1990, p. xv) observed: "In general, state departments of education have created only limited initiatives on behalf of students identified as having behavioral or emotional disabilities under the mandate of the EHA. Actions seem either reactive (i.e., to a court decision), limited in scope or non-existent. Under one half of the states even have full-time specialists in this area."

Although I do not believe that such collaborative agreements can result in long-range permanent services for youngsters with handicaps, their most significant effect so far has been in stimulating short-term demonstrations and experimental projects between local school districts and other human services and with business and industry. Unfortunately, most of these have been completely dependent on special grants and time-limited funding—for example, federal grants through P.L. 94-142 or the Carl D. Perkins Vocational Education Act. After the end of the demonstration or project period, only a few have been absorbed into the tax levy income base of the public school districts. In part, this has been because the school district has rarely been willing, or in a position, to pick up the costs of the other agency or business members of the collaboration, and these, too, have not been willing or able to continue their part of the funding.

FUNDING, FINANCING

One of the most complex issues involved in collaboration or integration of services is that of managing the funding or financing. Each component of the service usually involves a separate funding stream. As I have indicated, the education program is financed from state and local tax revenues, for the most part from real estate taxes, though in many states this is augmented from general state revenues. In some states there is additional income from state lotteries. To a limited extent, a state may be utilizing federal grants for projects in special education or vocational or career education, or federal "impact aid" (P.L. 81-815 and 81-874, as amended) to areas where military bases and government offices reduce local tax revenues while increasing the number of children to be educated. When the management of integrated services is not a local school district or a state agency, the managing agency must contract for these funds with the local or state agency, as the case may be.

The psychiatric treatment component of the program requires attention to another set of funding sources. A clinic, mental health center, or rehabilitation agency may be funded for its treatment and residential programs through a combination of contracts with local and/or state mental health authorities, substance abuse agencies, Medicaid payments, and fees from clients directly or through health insurance policies. Each funding stream has its own requirements as to timing (advance payments on a fiscal year basis, end of year basis as deficit financing, per capita payments, and so on); as to outcome standards (attendance and duration of participation, success in results, and so on); as to credentialing (agency's level of fiscal stability and reliability, credentials of professional and paraprofessional staff); and as to use of grant or contract (e.g., no comingling with other funds). Each supplier of financial support has its own requirements as to method of first applying or requesting renewal and for reports interim and final.

In addition to educational and treatment programs, an integrated program for mentally ill adolescents may have funding for residential care (from social services, human resources, mental health, criminal justice, youth services), and for training and work (from labor or services for youth and the like). These, too, have rules, regulations, standards, and reporting requirements of their own. One community mental health center director told me recently that he manages 16 sources of income for his child and adolescence program alone.

The methods of managing, one might almost say "juggling," such an array of funding are not unique to this field. Almost every program of health or human services has similar problems with which to cope. The methods and techniques involved are covered in texts on health and mental health administration. They call for knowledge and experience in business and public administration, without which many otherwise worthy human services fail.

THE SCHOOLS SEEKING COLLABORATION IN THE COMMUNITY

The examples I gave in Chapter 1 are illustrative of school districts acting alone. Other examples are given here:

The Dallas Independent School District (RRE, 1986) set up Project IMPACT in 1984 as part of its Special Education Department. Housed in a former elementary school building, the project provides evaluative and counseling services for severely disabled youth, mostly mentally retarded/developmentally disabled, but some seriously emotionally disturbed. Close contact is kept with parents through group conferences. To these are invited representatives of such community agencies as the local mental health/mental retardation authority, the local office of the state Division of Vocational Rehabilitation, the agencies serving the mentally retarded and the deaf, as well as the city parks and recreation department and some cooperative businesses. Plans are made for placement in work programs. The Project IMPACT staff create long-range goals for each student and arrange for close monitoring during the first month on the job or with the community agency and every 1 or 2 months thereafter until the student's eligibility for public school service ends. Preference is given to students who are nearing the end of their public school careers.

Project PASSAGE (RRE, 1984) was set up as part of a suburban school district on the edge of Houston, Texas, to provide transitional services for young adults in five independent school districts. A cooperating Agency Council includes membership from the five local education agencies, the Mental Health/Mental Retardation Authority of the county, the

Texas Rehabilitation Commission, the Adult Probation Office, and various local social services. The project, funded through a grant from the Texas Planning Council for Developmental Disabilities, provides vocational evaluations, a mixture of psychosocial services and counseling, training in activities of daily living, and job placement. Although its major interest is in youth who are mentally retarded/developmentally disabled, youth who are mentally ill or learning disabled are also served. Follow-up is provided through a maximum age of 25.

Some of the local school districts in California have developed special cooperative programs with the state Department of Rehabilitation. Three, which have been adjudged exemplary by the Regional Rehabilitation Network covering the western states (RRN, 1986), are the programs of the *Los Angeles Unified School District, the San Gabriel Valley Area School-to-Work Transition Program*, and the *Terrance High School/Department of Rehabilitation Cooperative Project*. In brief, the Department of Rehabilitation places counselors in the secondary schools to assist the students. Cooperatively with special education or career education, there is advice and guidance on vocational choice, work experience/trade training programs, services to parents, and job placement. Terrance High School supplies a full-time job development specialist; in the other schools the rehabilitation counselor uses local contacts. Follow-up is the responsibility of Department of Rehabilitation counselors. All disability groups are served, including the mentally ill.

Another exemplary school-based programs that has been demonstrating collaborative programs with its state division of vocational rehabilitation has been the *Cooperative Services*

Model (PEER, 1989) of the New York State Department of Education, centered on Staten Island, New York City. This program serves the learning disabled, the emotionally disturbed, the mentally retarded, and the multiply handicapped in all six high schools. The predominantly served group is the learning disabled. A team of occupational educator, special educator, and vocational rehabilitation counselor undertakes assessment, counseling, and guidance for the student and consultation as to curriculum planning and performance for classroom teachers. The Goodwill Industries is utilized under contract to supply work evaluation and, with the rehabilitation counselor, referrals to additional rehabilitation services and job placement. Follow-up after employment is by the Office of Vocational Rehabilitation for a period of 60 days.

Project A.L.I.V.E. (PEER, 1989) of the Avenel Learning Center, Woodbridge Township, New Jersey, School District, was designed specifically for high school students who were classified as emotionally disturbed. A special unit, known as the Avenel Learning Center, is an alternative high school program "based on the traditional high school curriculum with a vocational emphasis" (p. 2). Project A.L.I.V.E. provides crisis intervention, individual and group counseling, and a parent support group. There is also a career advisory committee, provision for vocational assessment, and an in-house manufacturing work experience in which the students make objects for sale. Close contact is kept with community resources. There is no provision for job placement except through the state vocational rehabilitation services and local agencies. Services end with completion of schooling.

For all the limitations of the Job Training Partnership Act in serving disabled persons (see Chapter 5), some schools have been able to take advantage of it to initiate programs for handicapped youth. For example, the Tri-SELPAS Job Project (RNN, 1986) links nine school districts in Contra Costa County, California, in a program funded under the JTPA. The services provided include vocational assessment, training in activities of daily living, and a computer-assisted remedial curriculum. High school juniors and seniors who are disabled are placed in paid short-term on-the-job training leading to permanent employment. An advisory council for the project includes membership from major employers, the Contra Costa County Private Industry Council, the state Department of Rehabilitation, special and vocational educators, community agencies, and parents. Although the project specializes in serving the mentally retarded/developmentally disabled, it also serves students who are severely emotionally disturbed or have serious learning disablement.

To an increasing extent, schools are developing direct collaborations with the business world to increase opportunities for adolescents with handicaps to make the transition to regular employment. For example, Knitzer and colleagues (1990) describe a collaborative program between the Manatee County Schools and Holiday Inn in which on-the-job training is afforded at the hotel for 11th- and 12th-grade special education students. "While involved in the program, the students are monitored daily by the on-the-job training teacher. When the training is completed and work criteria are satisfied, the student receives a certificate which lists all the job tasks that he has mastered. What makes this program special is the care with which the teacher works out jobs for the students that match their skills and potentials, and the fact that the hotel industry needs workers" (p. 84).

The High School of Fashion Industries in New York City has developed *Project RAGS* (Reaching Achievement through

Garment Studies) (PEER, 1989) in which it cooperates with various industries in New York's fashion center. Students are selected in their sophomore, junior, or senior year because they are demonstrating talent in fashion construction, textile design, illustration, display, or interior design. The disability groups served are learning disabled and emotionally disturbed. The students are assigned to positions in stock, merchandise control, publicity, customer service, and alterations, in the mornings, 5 days a week. Afternoons are reserved for vocational and academic instruction. Each group of 12 students is accompanied by a teacher, and "where appropriate," a paraprofessional. There is individual coaching on work tasks and work behavior at the job site, and assistance in job placement at graduation. There is no formal follow-up after graduation and job placement.

CHANGING THE EDUCATIONAL THRUST

As I have already indicated (see Chapter 3), increasing concern for the education of children who are handicapped has been accompanied by changing emphases in the education of all children. The most significant of these for the youngsters with whom we are here concerned have been the developments in application of career education and the recurring recommendations for infusing with vocational education the total curriculum for all children. There is also the suggestion, strongly advocated by some leading special educators, that training for all teachers would make possible the mainstreaming of almost all children who have handicaps as well as increasing educational opportunities for all children.

While there have been a great many developments in introducing elements of career education into elementary and secondary school curricula, the great emphases in career education curriculum building and establishment of state advisory panels on career education evaporated with the Reagan administration and the ending of its career education push. Vocational educators still believe that regular education would benefit greatly from what some refer to as total infusion and integration of "manual arts," but, as the tone of the New York City schools chancellor's letter implies (see Chapter 5), this philosophy is unlikely to get much support from educational administrators. So far as changing the total system so that what is good for disability becomes available for all, the prospects seem to me to be nil. The initial costs of application alone would be too great for most any school system to absorb, even if there were demonstrated proof, not now existent, that future experiences would result in sizable savings.

THE COMMUNITY SEEKING OUT SCHOOLS

Long before the current development by a number of businesses of cooperative programs with schools to increase opportunities for the movement of youth into higher education or employment, some organizations serving the handicapped established their own school-to-work collaborations. The societies for the mentally retarded/developmentally disabled spearheaded this effort, stimulated in great part by advocacy associations of parents and relatives of the disabled. Such programs, serving persons of a multiplicity of handicaps, have also managed to include some youngsters who are emotionally disturbed or learning disabled.

Goodwill Industries of Central Arizona has organized a cooperative program with the Phoenix Union High School District and the state departments of education and vocational rehabilitation "to serve students with severe mental, emotional and learning disabilities who have not been successful in traditional special education or alternative work experience programs" (RRN, 1988, Appendix A-b). Students receive work adjustment experience in the Goodwill salvage and sale facility and the development of an IEP (Individualized Education Program) at the school. While primary funding for the project comes from the state department of education, the "case management" is by Goodwill Industries.

Eden Express, in Haywood, California, was organized as a nonprofit commercial restaurant to serve as a center to help persons recovering from mental illness or other physical and mental disabilities reenter the employment market with saleable job skills (RRN, 1988). "Each individual advances at his or her own pace through job assignments such as dishwashing, laundry, janitorial, food preparation, waiting tables, or cashier. The five-month training program covers work adjustment techniques, job skills, academic skills, vocational planning, and job search" (Appendix C-b). Eden Express collaborates with the schools in the metropolitan-urban East San Francisco Bay area of California. It charges fees for service to the state department of education for services given to school students.

The program of Work, Inc., described in Chapter 1, is also an example of a community agency, in this case a general work- related rehabilitation center, offering its services to public school systems.

PSYCHIATRIC SERVICE APPROACHES

One facet of most services to persons with emotional disability does not appear to be much considered. This is the relapsing or recurring nature of many mental illnesses. Most approaches to disability or handicap assume there is a constant condition or one that might be bettered rather than one that might deteriorate. Although the terms "handicap" and "disability" are often used interchangeably, the World Health Organization (WHO, 1980) makes an important distinction that is often helpful in planning services. It categorizes conditions according to the limitations of the patient as disease or disorder, impairment, disability, and handicap:

> It is possible, under this classification, for one to have an impairment that does not lead to a recognized physical disability, such as asthma or allergic disturbances that show up only under unusual conditions. It is also possible for one to have a disability which does not constitute a handicap. Such a situation would hold with a leg amputee who, with a prosthesis, could continue a relatively normal life in a sedentary occupation. A handicap would exist in this instance, however, if even with the prosthesis the individual could not return to work involving heavy labor, much standing, or walking. (Black, 1988, p. 173)

These distinctions are at the root of the differences in approach to dealing with persons who are mentally ill. The medical or psychiatric approach focuses on treating and stabilizing the disorder or disease, recognizing there may be exacerbations, remissions, and relapses. The educational and vocational approaches assume a disability whose handicap might be lessened. Somehow these approaches must be brought together if there is to be collaboration beneficial to youngsters who are mentally ill. Only in recent years have service programs specifically for the mentally ill begun to focus their attention on combining educational and vocational resources with psychiatric treatment in addressing the problems of transition to adulthood. Consider these examples:

A Children's Psychiatric Institution (Knitzer et al., 1990, p. 71). The state psychiatric hospital for children in Rockland County, New York, north of New York City, began in 1974 to develop cooperative programs with local school systems. By 1990 the hospital provided mental health clinic services in 40 schools and day treatment programs in 27 schools in three counties. A very close working relationship exists with the Boards of Cooperative Educational Services (BOCES), and the collaborative program now shows interest in developing post-high school vocational programs. This excellent project has had a great effect in reducing hospitalization and increasing school attendance of emotionally disturbed, behaviorally disordered children. The move toward post-high school programming is in the right direction, but both the hospital and the schools are limited by the required move of patients to adult services on reaching the cut-off age of 22.

A Community Mental Health Center (Russert & Frey, 1991). The Program of Assertive Community Treatment (PACT), in Madison, Wisconsin, is a well-known, award-winning mental health service program. "Treatment and services include direct assistance with symptom monitoring and management, 24-hour crisis availability, facilitation of an optimally supportive environment, and direct assistance with instrumental functioning. Treatment objectives include the prevention of relapse or reduction of primary symptoms, increased satisfaction with life, lower subjective stress, and improved social and vocational functioning" (p. 9).

The vocational services of PACT include assessment, particularly situational assessment in a job setting and an array of prevocational, supported employment, and job placement opportunities. PACT differs from most mental health centers in utilizing a "life coach" model. It recognizes both that persons who are mentally ill may require a longer period of adjustment to reach full-time working level and that supportive services may be necessary through a variety of job attempts. "Motivation to work and congruence of goals between client and staff are thought to evolve over time, through the long-term treatment relationship. Inability to sustain employment or frequent job change does not result in termination from the vocational development process" (p. 10).

PACT enjoys a close collaborative relationship with other community agencies and with the state Division of Vocational Rehabilitation. The opportunities exist for special relationships with educational authorities to effect transition from school to work, but to my knowledge these have not been fully implemented.

A PSYCHOSOCIAL REHABILITATION CENTER

Thresholds, in Chicago, was established as a psychosocial club in the 1950s for persons discharged from mental hospitals. It is now one of the best established psychosocial rehabilitation programs in the world. In addition to in-house prevocational and recreational programs, over the years Thresholds has added transitional and supported work programs. Its philosophy includes considering participants in the program as "members" of the club, with ensuing rights and responsibilities (see Black, 1988, pp. 56-65). In 1972 Thresholds added a program for adolescents and young adults, aged 16 to 21 (Knitzer et al., 1990, pp. 84-85). Many of these members are very seriously mentally ill, most are receiving psychotropic medication, and all have been hospitalized at least once. The Bank Street College report describes the program for youth as follows:

> The program is carefully structured. First the youth have an in-house job, working on the kitchen crew and preparing meals for up to 100 people a day. Depending on their response this lasts for between three and 12 months. Then they are placed as a group in paid jobs. This group placement means the youth work with familiar peers. The program provides an on-the-site job coach. On-the-job education around drugs and medication, stress reduction techniques and social skills training within a specific context is also available. This in turn is followed by a paid job supervised by the employer. Finally, with the help of a job club, each student finds his or her own job, although access to support groups at Thresholds continues. Students meet once a week as a group, often engaging in leisure time activities. This is supplemented by a family participation program, and an employer involvement program which helps employers understand the unique needs of these young adults.

A "Community Scholar Program" was initiated at Thresholds in 1988 (Community Network News, 1990). This program is to assist youth with mental illness who have the

capacity for and interest in higher education to make successful transitions to college and then to employment. The program includes remedial education, tutoring assistance by
peers, linkage with postsecondary schools and colleges, a
support group, and a follow-along service while the students
are attending school and afterward. The students continue as
members of Thresholds with all of its advocacy and support
resources available to them. The Community Scholar Program is funded by a grant from the Office of Special Education
and Rehabilitative Services, U.S. Department of Education.

A TRAINING AND EMPLOYMENT CENTER

A unique vocational rehabilitation agency organized under
nonprofit auspices was established in Baltimore, Maryland, in
1986: S.T.E.P., Inc. (Schapiro Training and Employment
Program) (RRE, 1987) serves persons who have chronic
mental illness. Referrals come from the community mental
health and rehabilitation programs in the metropolitan Baltimore area. Services include orientation, vocational assessment, assignment to a job coach, development of a support
group, appointment to a job club, and finally placement in
supported employment in business or industry. The job coach,
in addition to doing training in specific work tasks, monitors
the individual's medication schedules and therapy sessions, as
well as performs many of the functions of a "case manager."
A weekly Work Retention Club is available in the evening on
an optional basis. In case of failure on the job, another
supported work assignment may be made, if the client is
motivated and judged by the staff of S.T.E.P. to be capable.
Funding for S.T.E.P. comes from the state department of

mental hygiene, the Office of Manpower Resources, and the state vocational rehabilitation agency.

WHAT WORKS?

It is tempting for one who is a health planner to take the components that Koroloff (1990) proposes as adequate transition policy and design a program mandating the roles and responsibilities that each collaborating element would carry. While such an ideal program can be designed, I would know as an administrator that it represented a goal unlikely ever to be achieved. Each of the examples so far described is a compromise, with limitations that reduce the efficacy of accomplishment for many of the youngsters it purports to serve.

Programs in which the school is the originator and the integrator, no matter how comprehensive, suffer from limitations in time. They are available only until the youngsters leave the school system or soon thereafter. The adjustments of former students to early adulthood and the work world are left untouched. Programs initiated and integrated by community agencies are limited in their control over the educational experience of the youngsters, and frequently by their lack of command of the treatment regimen.

A solution that is currently in vogue is the appointment of a "case manager" who acts to inform the youngster and the youth's family of the resources available—educational, vocational, treatment, recreational, and so on—and who serves as advocate to see that the services actually are provided. Case managers are used by mental health agencies, social service programs for children and youth, and a few school districts.

There are glowing anecdotal reports of the use of case managers, but many questions remain. It is unclear what training case managers require to be successful, whether professional preparation or an associate level degree or none at all is necessary. Could the services and advocacy promoted for case managers be subsumed under the duties and responsibilities of already existing staff, such as a social worker in a mental health center or a special education teacher? Should case managers have resources of their own, such as financial aid to offer in crises or even the ability to proffer short-term counseling or psychotherapy. It is too early to make judgments on these matters.

However, I consider that the greatest limitation to case management services for mentally ill youth is that they are bound by the limitations of the agency or school district they represent. The school case manager cannot continue services once the youngster has left school; the agency case manager cannot ensure educational services unless there is a collaborative agreement between the agency and the school district. As great a help as case management no doubt is, it alone is not a solution to bridging the period from schooling to work.

Of all the human service systems I have reviewed, the only ones that regularly, by structure, embrace the period between childhood and adulthood are those regarded as rehabilitative. For the mentally ill these include rehabilitation centers, psychosocial rehabilitation programs, community mental health centers, and centers for independent living. All of these but the community mental health centers automatically include the range of educational, vocational, and living services that can make transition from school to work a reality. However, it is not inconsistent with its mandate of psychiatric treatment for a community mental health center to have close collaboration with its school district and with the department of vocational rehabilitation and transitional work programs. Two such, with which I have had occasion to work closely, are the Community Mental Health Center of Rockland County, New York, and the Soundview-Throgs Neck Community Mental Health Center, in the Bronx. Both have children's and youth services, both have liaison counseling and treatment programs with their local school districts, and both have sheltered work and transitional work (including supported employment) with local business and industry. In all of these there are similarities to the PACT and Threshold programs just described.

For years I have been an advocate of "generalized" rehabilitation services, that is, programs open to a range of disabilities. It has seemed to me that specialized services, particularly those used in preparation for the workaday world, should not be reserved for only one disability group. The underlying desire is to ensure a more economic use of scarce resources. However, when it comes to designing programs for serving mentally ill youth, particularly the more seriously disabled, sharing programs with persons having other types of handicaps raises problems. The need for integrating psychiatric treatment with the educational program is specific to youngsters who are mentally ill, to an extent not present even with other chronic diseases. The aversion that the emotionally disturbed young people express to working alongside persons physically disabled, in work training or transitional work, presents another difficult issue. The fears and uncertainties faced even by staff experienced in dealing with the behavior

of persons who are physically handicapped or mentally retarded, but not with the exacerbations of mental illness,
greatly reduce the opportunities for youth with mental illness.

Therefore, I believe that in the present, and for some years
to come, it must be the responsibility of the mental health
services field to become the focal agency, the integrator of
transitional services from adolescence to adulthood for mentally ill youth. Building on the current developing interest in
psychiatric rehabilitation, psychosocial service centers, community mental health centers, and psychiatric institutions are
better able than the public schools or any other human service
agency to provide continuity of treatment and care during
these crucial years of adolescence and young adulthood, to
develop the kinds of agreements and collaboration needed
with schools and the workplace, and to supply the support and
advocacy the youngsters and families require. I do not propose
that there be any reduction in the efforts, demonstrations, or
experiments by the school systems or any other agencies. The
amount of need is so great and the range of disability so wide
that many youngsters can be helped by every type of program
I have herein presented. But for young people who are severely mentally ill, and who require complex educational
programming and treatment care, psychiatric rehabilitation
will have to become the future coordinator and monitor of
transition services.

REFERENCES

Achenbach, T. M. (1978). The Child Behavior Profile in Boys Aged 6 to 11. *Journal of Consulting and Clinical Psychology, 46,* 478–488.

Achenbach, T. M., McConaughy, S. H., & Howell, C. T. (1987). Child/Adolescent Behavioral and Emotional Problems: Implications of Cross–Informant Correlations for Situational Specificity. *Psychological Bulletin 101,* (1–3), January–May, 227–228.

Adelson, J. (1986). *Inventing Adolescence: The Political Psychology of Everyday Schooling.* New Brunswick, NJ: Transaction Books.

Aichorn, A. (1934). *Wayward Youth.* New York: Viking Press.

Alt, H. (1955). *Forging Tools for Mental Health.* Monograph No. 4. New York: Jewish Board of Guardians.

American Psychiatric Association. (1987). *Diagnostic and Statistical Manual of Mental Disorders* (3rd ed.—rev.). Washington, DC: Author.

Anthony, W. A., & Blanch, A. (1987). Supported Employment for Persons Who Are Psychiatrically Disabled: An Historical and Conceptual Perspective. *Psychosocial Rehabilitation Journal, XI*(2), October, 5–23.

Asarnow, J. R. (1988). Children at Risk for Schizophrenia: Converging Lines of Evidence. *Schizophrenia Bulletin. 14,* (4), 1,613.

Bandura, A. (1977). *Social Learning Theory.* Englewood Cliffs, NJ: Prentice Hall.

Bandura, A. (1980). The Stormy Decade: Fact or Fiction. in R. E. Muus (Ed.), *Adolescent Behavior and Society* (3rd ed.). New York: Random House.

Bandura, A., & Walters, R. M. (1963). *Social Learning and Personality Development.* New York: Holt, Rinehart & Winston.

Barreal, J. & Mack, J. (1979). Responsibilities of Regular Class-room Teachers for Handicapped Students. Fact Sheet, The Council for Exceptional Children. ERIC Document 179–034. Reston, VA: ERIC Clearinghouse on Handicapped and Gifted Children.

Barro, S. M. (1987). *Who Drops Out of High School/Findings from High School and Beyond*. Washington, DC: U.S. Government Printing Office.

Bauer, A., & Sapona, R. H. (1988). Facilitating Communication as a Basis for Intervention for Students with Severe Behavioral Disorders. *Behavioral Disorders, 13*(4), August. 280–287.

Beard, J. H. (1976). Psychiatric Rehabilitation at Fountain House. In J. Meislin (Ed.), *Rehabilitation Medicine and Psychiatry*. Springfield, IL: Charles C. Thomas.

Behar, L. B. (1984). An Integrated System of Services for Seriously Disturbed Children. Presented at the ADAMHA/OJJDP State of the Art Research on Juvenile Offenders with Serious Alcohol, Drug Abuse, and Mental Health Problems. Rockville, MD.

Bellamy, G. & Wilcox, B. (1981). *From Schools to What? Transition Services for Students with Severe Handicaps*. Eugene, OR: University of Oregon.

The Benchmark. (1989). Developmental Reports. The New York State Education Department. Vol. 9, No. 1, September, p. 9.

The Benchmark. (1990). A Bimonthly Report on Occupational Education in New York State. The New York State Education Department, September, p. 6.

Berryman, S. E. (1989). *Shadows in the Wings: The Next Educational Reform*. Occasional Paper No. 1. Presented to the New York State Council on Vocational Education, Albany, NY.

Black, B. J. (1970). *Principles of Industrial Therapy for the Mentally Ill*. New York: Grune and Stratton.

Black, B. J. (1971). Milieu Therapy. *Encyclopedia of Social Work, 1*(16), 844–851.

Black, B. J. (1988). *Work and Mental Illness: Transitions to Employment*. Baltimore, MD: Johns Hopkins University Press.

Blos, P. (1941). *The Adolescent Personality*. New York: Appleton–Century Co.

Blos, P. (1979). *The Adolescent Passage: Developmental Issues.* New York: International Universities Press.

BOCES. (1989). *The Vocational Assessment of Students with Handicapping Conditions: Definition and Programmatic Guidelines.* Prepared by the Cooperative Services Model Project, BOCES 2, Suffolk County, in cooperation with the New York State Education Department. Albany, NY: Office for Education of Children with Handicapping Conditions.

Brandenburg, N. A., Friedman, R. M., and Silver, S. E. (1989). The Epidemiology of Childhood Psychiatric Disorders: Prevalence Findings from Recent Studies. *Journal of Child and Adolescent Psychiatry, 29*(1).

Brodsky, C. M. (1987). Factors Influencing Work–Related Disability. In A. T. Myerson, & T. Fine (Eds.), *Psychiatric Disability: Clinical, Legal, and Administrative Dimensions.* Washington, DC: American Psyciatric Press.

Business Week. (1988). Human Capital: The Decline of America's Work Force. Special Report, September 19.

Caplan, P. J., & Hall–McCorquodale, I. (1983). Mother-Blaming in Major Clinical Journals. *American Journal of Orthopsychiatry, 55*(3).

The Chancellor's Advisory Mainstreaming Oversight Committee. (1987). *A Plan for Effective Mainstreaming in the Community School Districts.* Unpublished manuscript.

Cleary, E. J. (1990). The Changing Face of Labor in the Year 2001. *NY Works.* New York State Department of Labor. Winter.

Cole, P. F. (1989). *The New American Worker.* A discussion paper prepared for a conference presented by the New York Senate on Policy Options and Stategies for Labor Shortages. Buffalo, NY, September 11.

Collegebound—Final Report. (1987). Evaluation. Winchester Public Schools. Winchester, MA, February.

Community Network News. (1990). Models of Supported Education for Young Adults with Psychiatric Disabilities. Center for Psychiatric Rehabilitation, Boston University. Vol. 6, No. 3, February.

Conners, C. K. (1973). Rating Scales for Use in Drug Studies with Children. *Psychopharmacology Bulletin*, Special Issue, No. 24, 24–84.

Contemporary Education. (1978). The Ten Commandments for Freedom in the Classroom, Vol. XLVI, No. 4. Indiana School of Education.

Cornes, P. (1987). Vocational Rehabilitation for Tomorrow's World: A British View. In D. E. Woods, & D. Vandergoot (Eds.), *The Changing Nature of Work, Society and Disability: The Impact on Rehabilitation Policy.* New York: World Rehabilitation Fund.

Corthell, D. W., & VanBoskirk, C. (1984). *Continuum of Services: School to Work.* Report from study group. Eleventh Institute on Rehabilitation Studies, San Antonio, TX, June. Menomonie, WI: Research and Training Center, Stout Vocational Rehabilitation Institute, University of Wisconsin–Stout.

Council for Exceptional Children. (1979). *Fact Sheets from the ERIC Clearinghouse on Handicapped and Gifted Children.* 1979 Series. Information Center on Exceptional Children. Reston VA: ERIC Clearinghouse on Handicapped and Gifted Children. ERIC Document 179–034.

Daniels, L. A. (1988). Changes in Special Education Urged. *The New York Times*, Feb. 5, p. B5.

Danielson, L. C., & Bellamy, G. T. (1987). *State Variation in Placement of Children with Handicaps in Segregated Environments.* Unpublished manuscript. Office of Special Education Programs, New York State Department of Education.

deAnda, D. (1987). Adolescents. *Encyclopedia of Social Work* (18th ed., Vol. 1, pp. 51–67). Washington, DC: National Association of Social Workers.

Dick, M. (1985). *A Comprehensive Model: Vocational Preparation for Learning Disabled and Behaviorally Disordered Students.* ERIC Document 265–727.

Dunham, D. B. (1986). *Synthesis of Recent Research on Positive Outcomes of High School Vocational Education.* The Oregon Alliance for Program Improvement, Oregon State University, Corvallis, OR. Presented to the National Council on Vocational Education, October 1, Columbus, OH.

D'Zamko, M. E., & Hedges, W. D. (1985). *Helping Exceptional Students Succeed in the Regular Classroom.* West Nyack, NY: Parker Publishing.

Eaves, R. C. (1982). A Proposal for the Diagnosis of Emotional Disturbance. *The Journal of Special Education, 16*(4), 463.

Education for All Handicapped Children's Act. (1975). P. L. 94–142.

Erikson, E. H. (1950). *Childhood and Society.* New York: W.W. Norton.

Erikson, E. H. (1963). *Childhood and Society.* (2nd ed). New York: W.W. Norton.

ESEA. (1965). *Part B. Title I. Elementary and Secondary Education Act*, as amended. P.L. 89–10, P.L. 89–313, P.L. 90–247, P.L. 91–230, P.L. 93–380, and P.L. 95–561. U.S. Code: 20 U.S.C. 24c(a) (5). C.F.D.A.: 13.427.

Esman, A. H. (1992). Treatment and Services for Adolescents. *Hospital and Community Psychiatry, 43*(6), 616–639.

Evans, P. L. (1979). *Classification and Labeling Issues: Toward Operationalizing Legal Definitions of Handicapping Conditions.* Presented at the Annual Convention of the American Psychological Association, September 1, New York. ERIC Document 181–628. National Institute of Education, U.S. Department of Health, Education and Welfare.

Fabian, E., & Wiedefeld, M. F. (1989). Supported Employment for Severely Psychiatrically Disabled Persons: A Descriptive Study. *Psychosocial Rehabilitation Journal, 13*(2), October, 53–60.

Fair Labor Standards Act, as amended. P.L. 89–601, P.L. 95–151, P.L. 101–157 (amendments of 1989). U.S. Code: 29 U.S.C. 203.

Fairweather, J. S. (1989). Transition and Other Services for Handicapped Students in Local Education Agencies. *Exceptional Children, 55*(4), 315–320.

Feinstein, S. C. (Guest Ed.). (1980). *Adolescence: Perspectives on Psychotherapy. New Directions for Mental Health Services.* San Francisco, CA: Jossey–Bass.

Feis, P., & Werbel, V. (1983). *The Cooperative Vocational Program.* Educational Service Unit #9, Hastings, NE. Office of Special Education and Rehabilitative Services, U.S. Department of Education, Grant No. G00–800–1724. ERIC Document 242–483.

Forness, S. R., & Kavale, K. A. (1988). Psychopharmacologic Treatment: A Note on Classroom Effects. *Journal of Learning Disabilities, 21*(3), March, 144–147.

Freud, A. (1937). *The Ego and the Mechanics of Defense.* New York: Hogarth Press.

Friedenberg, E. Z. (1987). Extracurricular Activities. Review of Greenberger, E. & Steinberg, L. (1986). *When Teenagers Work: The Psychological and Social Costs of Adolescent Employment.* New York: Basic Books. In *Readings—A Journal of Reviews and Commentary in Mental Health, 2*(2), June, American Orthopsychiatric Association.

Friedman, R., & Duchnowski, A. (1987). Severely Emotionally Disturbed Children and P.L. 94–142. *Newsletter*, Division of Child, Youth, and Family Services, American Psychological Association, 10(3), 2–3.

Friedman, R. M., Silver, S. E., Duchnowski, A. J., Kutash, K., Eisen, M., Brandenburg, N. A., & Prange, M. (1988). *Characteristics of Children with Serious Emotional Disturbances Identified by Public Systems as Requiring Services.* No. 505, Research and Training Center for Children's Mental Health, Florida Mental Health Institute, University of South Florida, Tampa, FL. Unpublished manuscript.

Fromm, E. (1948). *Man for Himself.* New York: Farrar and Rinehart.

Fromm, E. (1955). *The Sane Society.* New York: Rinehart & Co.

GAO. (1991). *Job Training Partnership Act: Youth Participant Characteristics and Outcomes.* Briefing Report to Congressional Requesters. GAO/HRD-90-46-BR. January. Washington, DC: United States General Accounting Office.

Garnett, K., & Gerber, P. (1985). *Life Transitions of Learning Disabled Adults: Perspectives from Several Countries.* Monograph No. 32. International Exchange of Experts and Information in Rehabilitation. New York: World Rehabilitation Fund.

Gartner, A. (1986). *Reflections on Transition Model Programs for Youth with Disabilities.* The New York Area Study Group on Transition. Center for Advanced Study in Education (CASE). Graduate School, City University of New York.

Gearheart, B. R. (1967). *Administration of Special Education.* Springfield, IL: Charles C. Thomas.

Gellman, W., Gendel, H., Glaser, N. M., Friedman, S. B., & Neff, W. S. (1955). *Adjusting People to Work.* Monograph No. 1. Chicago, IL: Jewish Vocational Service and Employment Center.

Ginsburg, S. W. (1963). *A Psychiatrist's View on Social Issues.* New York: Columbia University Press.

Goldhaber, S. B. (1991). Summer Day Treatment for Children with Attention–Deficit Hyperactivity Disorder. *Hospital and Community Psychiatry, 42*(4), April, 422–424.

Goleman, D. (1989). Pioneering Studies Find Surprisingly High Rate of Mental Ills in Young. *The New York Times*, Science section, Tuesday, Jan. 10.

Gould, M. S., Wunsch–Hitzig, R., & Dehrenwend, B. (1981). Estimating the Prevalence of Childhood Psychopathology. *Journal of the American Academy of Child Psychiatry, 20*, 462–476.

Gralnick, A., Gantz, J., & Caton, C. L. M. (1986). The Young Adult Chronic Patient: Comparative Analyses. *The Psychiatric Journal of the University of Ottawa, II*(1), March.

Hall, G. S. (1904). *Adolescence: Its Psychology and Its Relations to Physiology, Anthropology, Sociology, Sex, Crime, Religion, and Education* (Vols. 1 & 2). New York: D. Appleton–Century Co.

Hall, R. H. (1986). *Dimensions of Work.* Beverly Hills, CA: Sage Publications.

Hartmann, E., Glasser, B. A., Greenblatt, M., Solomon, M. H., & Levinson, D. J. (1968). *Adolescents in a Mental Hospital.* New York: Grune & Stratton.

Hartnett, T. F. (1990). Facing the Changes. *NY Works*, New York State Department of Labor, Winter.

Hegenauer, J. (1988). *Evaluation of State of California Department of Education WorkAbility I Project 1986–1987.* Special Education Division, Sacramento, CA, June 27. Unpublished manuscript.

Herron, M. (1981). Youth Employment as a Preventive Mental Health Strategy. In J. S. Gordon, & M. Beyer, (Eds.), *Reaching Troubled Youth, Runaways and Community Mental Health.*

N.I.M.H., U.S. Department of Health and Human Services. D.H.H.S. Publication No. (ADM)81–955.

Hodgkinson, H. (1986). Guess Who's Coming to Work? *Occasional Paper No. 116.* The National Center for Research in Vocational Education. Columbus, OH: The Ohio State University.

Hoffman, M. L. (1980). Moral Development in Adolescence. In J. Adelson (Ed.), *Handbook of Adolescent Psychology.* New York: John Wiley.

Hospital and Community Psychiatry. (1991). Special Report: Highlights of the 42nd Institute on Hospital and Community Psychiatry. Vol. 42, No. 1, January.

Hoyt, K. B. (1975). *Career Education: Contributions to an Evolving Concept.* Salt Lake City, UT: Olympus Publishing.

Hoyt, K. B., Evans, R. N., Mackin, E. G., & Magnum, G. L. (1976). *Career Education: What It Is and How To Do It.* (2nd ed.). Salt Lake City, UT: Olympus Publishing.

ICD. (1989). *The ICD Survey III: A Report Card on Special Education.* Conducted for the International Center for the Disabled in Cooperation with the National Council on Disability by Louis Harris and Associates, New York.

Illinois Office of Education. (1979). *The Illinois Primer on Individualized Education Programs.* Springfield, IL: Department of Specialized Educational Services and Illinois Regional Resource Center, State Board of Education.

International Association of Psychosocial Rehabilitation Services. (1992). *PSR Connection.* p. 3.

Johnston, R. B. (1987). *Learning Disabilities, Medicine and Myth: A Guide to Understanding the Child and the Physician.* A College Hill Publication. Boston: Little, Brown.

Jones, M. (1953). *The Therapeutic Community.* New York: Basic Books.

Jureidini, J. (1991). Rehabilitation of Young Adolescents Severely Disabled After Psychosis: A Clinical Study. *Psychosocial Rehabilitation Journal, 14*(3), January, 104–109.

Kaplan, L. J. (1984). *Adolescence: The Farewell to Childhood.* New York: Simon and Schuster.

Kephart, N. C. (1968). *Learning Disability: An Educational Adventure.* West Lafayette, IN: Kappa Delta Pi Press.

Knitzer, J., Steinberg, Z.; & Fleisch, B. (1990). *At The Schoolhouse Door: An Examination of Programs and Policies for Children with Behavioral and Emotional Problems*. New York: Bank Street College of Education.

Koroloff, N. M. (1990). Moving Out: Transition Policies for Youth with Serious Emotional Disabilities. *The Journal of Mental Health Administration, 17*(1), Spring, 81.

Kounin, J. S., Friesen, W. V., & Norton, E. (1966). Managing Emotionally Disturbed Children in Regular Classrooms. *Journal of Educational Psychology, 57*, 1–13.

Kuhlen, R. G. (1952). *The Psychology of Adolescent Behavior Development*. New York: Harper and Brothers.

Lamb, H. R. (1987). Incentives and Disincentives of Disability Insurance for the Chronically Mentally Ill. In: A. T. Meyerson, & T. Fine (Eds.), *Psychiatric Disability: Clinical, Legal, and Administrative Dimensions*. Washington, DC: American Psychiatric Press.

Legislative Brief. (1988). The Forgotten Half Urges Major New Funding. The William T. Grant Commission on Work, Family and Citizenship. Washington, DC, Friday, Nov. 18.

Letter from Joseph A. Fernandez, Chancellor, New York City Public Schools, to Ms. Margaret Regan, Chairperson, Advisory Council for Occupational Education, July 30, 1990.

Links, P. S. (1983). Community Surveys of the Prevalence of Childhood Psychiatric Disorders: A Review. *Child Development. 54*, 544.

Margalit, M. (1989). Academic Competence and Social Adjustment of Boys with Learning Disabilities and Boys with Behavior Disorders. *Journal of Learning Disabilities, 22*(1), January, 41–45.

McIntyre, T. C., & Brulle, A. R. (1989). The Effectiveness of Various Types of Teacher Direction with Students Labeled Behavior Disordered. *Academic Therapy*, Teacher Directions, Vol. 25, No. 2, November, pp. 123–131.

McKinney, J. D. (1989). Longitudinal Research on the Behavioral Characteristics of Children with Learning Disorders. *Journal of Learning Disabilities, 22*(3), January, 141–150.

Messerer, J., & Meyers, G. (1983). *The Adequacy of High School Preparation on the Adult Adjustment of Learning Disabled*

Youth. ERIC Document 248–681. Reston, VA: Educational Resources Information Center.

Modrcin, M. J. (1988). Emotionally Handicapped Youth in Transition: Issues and Principles for Program Development. Research and Training Center, Regional Research Institute, Portland State University, Portland, OR. Unpublished manuscript.

Munich, R. L., & Glinberg, T. (1988). The Psychodynamics of Work. In: J. A. Ciardiello, & M. D. Bell (Eds.), *Vocational Rehabilitation of Persons with Prolonged Psychiatric Disorders.* Baltimore: Johns Hopkins Univerity Press.

Munroe, R. L. (1955). *Schools of Psychoanalytic Thought.* New York: Dryden Press.

NARF (National Association of Rehabilitation Facilities). (1988). Transitioning to Supported Employment: A Voice of Experience. *Voc/Dev Management Review, 5*(8), August, 5.

NARF. (1989). *Medical Management Review, 6*(8), August, 5.

NARF. (1990a). *Rehabilitation Review, 7*(5), January 29, 1–2.

NARF. (1990b). *Vocational/Developmental Rehabilitation Review, 7*(39), October 1.

NARF. (1991a). *Vocational/Developmental Issues Brief.* Issue 6. Civil Rights—The Americans with Disabilities Act. February 1.

NARF. (1991b). *Vocational/Developmental Rehabilitation Review, 8*(15), April 15.

NARF. (1991c). *Vocational/Developmental Rehabilitation Review, 8*(19), May 13.

National Association of State Boards of Education. (1979). *Answering Your Questions About P.L. 94–142 and Section 504: A Resource Handbook.* Washington, DC: National Association of State Directors of Special Education.

National Rehabilitation Association. (1992). Update Washington. *NRA Newsletter,* p. 8.

Neel, R. S. (1978). Research Findings Regarding the Use of Punishment Procedures with Severely Disordered Children. In: F. H. Wood, & K. C. Lakin (Eds.). *Punishment and Aversive Stimulation in Special Education: Legal, Theoretical and Practical Issues in their Use with Emotionally Disturbed Children and Youth.* Minneapolis, MN: Advanced Institute for Trainers of Teachers for Seriously Emotionally Disturbed Children and Youth. Department of Psychoeducational Studies, University of Minnesota. Reprinted by the Council for Exceptional Children, Reston, VA, 1982.

Neff, W. S. (1968). *Work and Human Behavior*. New York: Atherton Press.

Nelson, N. (1971). *Workshops for the Handicapped in the United States: An Historical and Developmental Perspective*. Springfield, IL: Charles C. Thomas.

Newsbrief. (1988–89). Office for Education of Children with Handicapping Conditions, New York State Department of Education. Vol. XII, No. 1.

New York City. (1987). *Special Education: A Call for Quality*. Report to the Mayor of the City of New York. Commission for Students with Handicapping Conditions, Advisory Council for Occupational Education, New York City Board of Education.

New York City Board of Education. (1984). *Educational Services for Children with Handicapping Conditions*. Division of Special Education/Division of High Schools.

New York State Council on Vocational Education. (1987). *Briefing Paper for Consideration of the Technical Committee on Occupational Education and the Handicapped*. September 14, Albany, NY.

New York State Council on Vocational Education. (1989). *Students with Disabling Conditions: Occupational Education Students with Disabling Conditions*. The ninth in a series of special reports. Albany, NY: Council on Vocational Education.

New York State Education Department. (1987a). The State of Learning and Working. *The Benchmark, 7*(2), November, 3. Office of Occupational and Continuing Education.

New York State Education Department. (1987b). Education and Economic Development. *Capsule Report*, p. 17. Albany, NY: Office of Occupational and Continuing Education.

New York State Education Department. (1989). *Students at Risk: An Occupational Education Perspective*. Albany, NY: Office of General and Occupational Education.

New York State Education Department. (1990). *SEEDS: News Release. Career Success Magazine.* Office of General and

Occupational Education. 90–14–SD–B.

New York State Education Law. (1979). *Amendment to the Regulations of the Commissioner of Education.* P. 200, Sec. 200.it.

New York Times. (1988). Changes in Special Education Urged. Section B. Feb. 3. p. 5.

New York Times. (1991). Schools Are Not Families. Editorial page, Monday, March 4.

NIMH (National Institute of Mental Health). (1981). The Kauai Longitudinal Study. *Science Reports: Adolescence and Stress.* (pp. 129–140). Washington, DC: Author.

Noble, J. H, & Collignon, F. C. (1987). System Barriers to Supported Employment for Persons with Chronic Mental Illness. *Psychosocial Rehabilitation Journal, VI*(2), October, 33.

Oakes, J. (1986). Beyond Tinkering: Reconstructing Vocational Education. In: G. Copa, J. Plihal, & M. Johnson (Eds.), *Revisioning Vocational Education in the Secondary School.* St. Paul, MN: University of Minnesota.

OECD. (1990). Active Life for Young People with Disabilities: Managing Transition to Adult Working Life. *International Policy Symposium on the Employment of Persons with Disabilities.* Room Document No.3. Centre for Educational Research and Innovation, Organisation for Economic Co–operation and Development. Paris, May 23. Unpublished manuscript.

Offer, D., Ostrov, E., & Howard, K. I. (Eds.). (1986). *Patterns of Adolescent Self–Image.* San Francisco: Jossey–Bass.

Offer, D., Ostrov, E., Howard, K. I., & Atkinson, R. (1988). *The Teenage World: Adolescent's Self–Image in Ten Countries.* New York: Plenum.

Parsons, T. (1950). Psychoanalysis and the Social Structure. *The Psychoanalytic Quarterly, 19,* July, 378–379.

Pearson, G. H. J. (1958). *Adolescence and the Conflict of Generations: An Introduction to Some of the Psychoanalytic Contributions to the Understanding of Adolescence.* New York: W. W. Norton.

PEER. (1989). *Catalogue of Exemplary Programs.* Programs that are Exemplary in Education and Rehabilitation. Research and Training Institute, National Center on Employment and Disability. Albertson, NY: Human Resources Center.

Petr, C. G., & Spano, R. N. (1990). Evolution of Social Services for Children with Emotional Disorders. *Social Work, 35*(3), 228–234.

Piaget, J., & Inhelder, B. (1958). *The Growth of Logical Thinking from Childhood to Adolescence* (A. Parsons & S. Seagrin, Trans.) New York: Basic Books.

P. L. 89–601. National League of Cities, et al., vs. Usery.

P. L. 94–142. Code: 20 U.S.C. 1411–1451. C.F.D.A. 13.443–13.586.

P. L. 101–336. *Americans with Disabilities Act of 1990.* 104 Stat. 101st Congress.

P. L. 101–508. *Omnibus Budget Reconciliation Act of 1990.*

President's Committee on Employment of People with Disabilities. 1990. *Fact Sheet on Supported Employment.* Washington, DC.

Quay, H. C. (1986). Conduct Disorders. In: H. C. Quay, & J. S. Werry, (Eds.), *Psychopathological Disorders of Childhood.* New York: John Wiley.

Rafalli, M. L. (1990). The Learning Disabled: Challenge to Identify. *The New York Times.* Sec. 12, Long Island Weekly, Oct. 7.

Redick, R. W., & Witkin, M. J. (1983). *Residential Treatment Centers for Emotionally Disturbed Children, United States, 1977–78 and 1979–80.* Washington, DC: National Institute of Mental Health.

Regional Centers include: Youth in Transition Project, Research and Training Center to Improve Services for Emotionally Handicapped Children and Their Families, Graduate School of Social Work, Portland State University, Portland, OR; California Assessment System for Adults with Learning Disabilities, California Community Colleges, Sacramento, CA; Bureau of Occupational Education Program Development, State Department of Education, Albany, NY; Rehabilitation Network of New England, The Network, Andover, MA; Regional Rehabilitation Network, Human Interaction Research Institute, Los Angeles, CA; The S.M.A.R.T. Exchange, Atlanta, GA; Southwest Educational Development Laboratory, Regional Rehabilitation Exchange, Austin, TX; PEER Regional Network, National Center on Employment and Disability, Human Resources Center, Albertson, NY; The New York Area Study Group on Transition,

Center for the Advanced Study in Education, The Graduate
School and University Center of the City University of New
York.

Report. (1990). Research and Training Center, Portland State
University, Portland, OR.

Rittenhouse, R. K. (1980). *The Bartley–Daly Act: Regulations for
the Implementation of Chapter 766 of the Acts of 1972: The
Comprehaensive Special Education Law of the Commonwealth
of Massachusetts: An Analysis Within the Context of Public Law
94–142*. Normal, IL: Illinois State University.

Rogers, C., & Farrow, F. (1983). *Effective State Strategies to
Promote Interagency Collaboration*. A Report of the Handi-
capped Public Policy Analysis Project. Washington, DC: The
Center for the Study of Social Policy. ERIC Document 245–467.

Rosenthal, T. L., & Zimmerman, B. J. (1978). *Social Learning and
Cognition*. New York: Academic Press.

RRE. (1984). *Klein ISD: Project PASSAGE*. Regional Rehabilitation Exchange, Southwest Educational Developmental Laboratory, Austin, TX., November.

RRE. (1986). *Dallas Independent School District: Project Impact:
Innovative Model Project for Achieving Community Transition*.
Regional Rehabilitation Exchange, Southwest Educational De-
velopmental Laboratory, Austin, TX.

RRE. (1987). *S.T.E.P., Inc*. Regional Rehabilitation Network,
Southwest Educational Developmental Laboratory, Austin, TX,
September.

RRN. (1986). *School-to-Work Transition Program*. RRN Innovation Directory. Regional Rehabilitation Network, Los Angeles,
CA. RRN Publication No. 3–09.

RRN. (1988). *School-to-Work Transition Programs*. (Becker T.
E., & Trotter, M. W., Eds.). Regional Rehabilitation Network,
Human Information Research Institute, Los Angeles, CA.

Rusch, F. R., & Phelps, L. A. (1987). Secondary Special Education
and Transition from School to Work: A National Priority.
Exceptional Children, 53(6), 488.

Russell, S. C., & Williams, E. C. (1984). *Teachers of the Behaviorally Disordered: Discrepancies Between Training and Perceived Needs*. Department of Special Education, Bowling Green

State University, Bowling Green, OH. ERIC Document 246–585. National Institute of Education, U.S. Department of Education.

Russert, M. G., & Frey, J. L. (1991). The PACT Vocational Model: A Step Into the Future. *Psychosocial Rehabilitation Journal, 14*(4), April, 7–18.

Rutherford, R. B., Jr. (1978). Theory and Research on the Use of Aversive Procedures in the Education of Moderately Behaviorally Disordered and Emotionally Disturbed Children and Youth. In: F. H. Wood, & K. C. Lakin, (Eds.). *Punishment and Aversive Stimulation in Special Education: Legal, Theoretical and Practical Issues in Their Use with Emotionally Disturbed Children and Youth.* Minneapolis, MN: Advanced Institute for Trainers of Teachers for Seriously Emotionally Disturbed Children and Youth, Department of Psychoeducational Studies, University of Minnesota. Reprinted by the Council for Exceptional Children, Reston, VA, 1982.

Sandell, S. H. (1988). *Who is Served in JTPA Programs: Patterns of Participation and Intergroup Equity.* National Commission for Employment Policy and Kalman Rupp, WESTAT, Inc. RR–88–03, Washington, DC.

Science. (1989). Computers Make Slow Progress in Class. News and Comment, Vol. 244, May 26.

Science. (1991). Assessing High School Achievement. Briefings, Vol. 251, Feb. 1, pp. 516–517.

Science Focus. (1988). Technology's Impact on the Work Force and Job Content. Vol.3, No.2, Fall, pp 1, 12. The New York Academy of Sciences.

Seidenberg, P. L. (1986). *A Framework for Curriculum Development for Secondary Learning Disabled Students.* Position Paper Series. Document No.3. Long Island University Transition Project: Learning How to Learn: A High School/College Linkage Model to Expand Higher Educational Opportunities for Learning Disabled Students. Brooklyn, NY: Long Island University. Unpublished manuscript.

Shore, K. (1986). *The Special Education Handbook: A Comprehensive Guide for Parents and Educators.* New York: Teachers College Press, Columbia University.

Srole, L. (1962). *Mental Health in the Metropolis: The Midtown Manhattan Study.* New York: McGraw Hill.

Stroul, B. A., & Friedman, R. M. (1986). *A System of Care for Severely Emotionally Disturbed Children and Youth.* Washington, DC: CASSP Technical Assistance Center, Georgetown University Child Development Center.

Supported Education. (1990). Center for Psychiatric Rehabilitation, Sargent College of Allied Health Professions, Boston University, Boston, MA. *Community Support Network News. 6*(3), February.

Taylor, D. B. (1978). *Implementation of the Individualized Education Program: A Teacher's Perspective.* Mideast Regional Resource Center, George Washington University, Washington, DC, in cooperation with the Division of Special Education and Student Support Systems, West Virginia Department of Education. ERIC Document 181–633. National Institute of Education, U.S. Department of Health, Education and Welfare.

Times Union. (1988). Business. Federal Job Training: a Mixed Review. Sunday, Oct. 9.

Tindall, L. W. (1981). *Vocational Education Models for Linking Agencies Serving the Handicapped. Technical Assistance Report.* U.S. Department of Education, Office of Adult and Vocational Education. ERIC Document 218–525. National Institute of Education, September 1.

Ullman, R. K., Sleator, E. K., & Sprague, R. L. (1984). A New Rating Scale for Diagnosis and Monitoring of ADD Children. *Psychopharmacology Bulletin, 20*, 160–163.

Unger, K. V. (1990). Supported Education for Young Adults with Psychiatric Disabilities. Center for Psychiatric Rehabilitation, Boston University. *Community Network News, 6*(3).

Unions. (1990). *Working People: Supported Employment and Labor Unions.* A Project of Service Employees International Union, Local 6, and Washington Supported Employment Initiative. Seattle, WA.

U.S. Department of Education. (1986). *Eighth Annual Report to Congress on the Implementation of the Education of the Handicapped Act.* Washington, DC: U.S. Office of Special Education and Rehabilitative Services.

U.S. Department of Education. (1980). *Summary of Existing Legislation Relating to the Handicapped.* Publication No. E–80–

20202. Washington, DC: Office of Special Education and Rehabilitative Services, Office for Handicapped Individuals.

U.S. Department of Labor. (1963). *Manpower Report of the President and a Report on Manpower Requirements, Resources, Utilization, and Training.* Washington, DC: U.S. Government Printing Office.

U.S. Department of Labor. (1989). *Work Based Learning: Training America's Workers.* Reference to: *The Forgotten Half: Pathways to Success for America's Youth and Young Families.* Washington, DC; The W.T. Grant Foundation.

Wehlage, G., Stone, C., Lesko, N., Nauman, C., & Page, R. (1982). *Effective Programs for the Marginal High School Student: A Report to the Wisconsin Governor's Employment and Training Office.* Wisconsin Center for Education Research, University of Wisconsin–Madison, Madison, WI. ERIC Document 222–452.

Wehman, P., Kregel, J., & Barcus, J. M. (1985). From School to Work: A Vocational Transition Model for Handicapped Students. *Exceptional Children, 52*(1), 25–37.

Weintraub, F. J. (1987). The Nation's Handicapped Children: How Have They Fared in the Public Education System? P.L. 94–142—A Decade of Progress. Division of Child, Youth, and Family Services, American Psychological Association. *Newsletter, 10*(3), 1.

Weiss, G. (1976). The Natural History of Hyperactivity in Childhood: *International Journal of Mental Health, 4,* 213–226.

Wheelis, A. (1953). *The Quest For Identity.* New York: Norton.

WHO. (1980). *International Classification of Impairments, Disabilities, and Handicaps: A Manual of Classification Relating to Disease.* New York: World Health Organization.

Wood, F. H., & Lakin, K. C. (Eds.). (1982). *Disturbing, Disordered or Disturbed? Perspectives on the Definition of Problem Behavior in Educational Settings.* Reston, VA: The Council for Exceptional Children.

World Almanac and Book of Facts. (1991). New York: World Almanac.

INDEX